George Shaw, Frederick Polydore Nodder, Richard P Nodder

The naturalists' miscellany, or, Coloured figures of natural objects; drawn and described immediately from nature

George Shaw, Frederick Polydore Nodder, Richard P Nodder

The naturalists' miscellany, or, Coloured figures of natural objects; drawn and described immediately from nature

ISBN/EAN: 9783743423770

Manufactured in Europe, USA, Canada, Australia, Japa

Cover: Foto ©ninafisch / pixelio.de

Manufactured and distributed by brebook publishing software (www.brebook.com)

George Shaw, Frederick Polydore Nodder, Richard P Nodder

The naturalists' miscellany, or, Coloured figures of natural objects; drawn and described immediately from nature

VIRO CELEBERRIMO

THOMÆ PENNANT

ARMIGERO,

NATURÆ INDEFESSO INDAGATORI,

CUJUS

STUDIO ET ACUMINE

PHYSICIS

TUM EXTERIS

TUM PRÆCIPUE NOSTRATIBUS
PROVECTIOR, ORNATIOR, LOCUPLETIOR,
TRADITA EST SCIENTIA,

QUARTUM HUNC

NATURÆ VIVARII

FASCICULUM,

D. D. D.

GEORGIUS SHAW,
FREDERICUS P. NODDER.

TO

THOMAS PENNANT

ESQUIRE,

FROM WHOSE LITERARY LABOURS

NATURAL HISTORY IN GENERAL,

AND THAT OF

GREAT BRITAIN IN PARTICULAR,

HAS RECEIVED SUCH AMPLE IMPROVEMENTS,

THIS FOURTH VOLUME

OF THE

NATURALIST's MISCELLANY

IS

WITH MUCH RESPECT INSCRIBED,

BY

HIS MOST OBEDIENT HUMBLE SERVANTS,

GEORGE SHAW,
FREDERICK P. NODDER.

PIPRA PUNCTATA.

Character Genericus.

Rostrum capite brevius, basi subtrigonum, integerrimum, apice incurvum.
Pedes gressorii.

Lin. Syst. Nat. p. 338.

Character Specificus.

PIPRA grisea, fusco undulata, vertice alisque nigris, albo punctatis, tectricibus caudæ rubris.

Femina? minus vivida, capite maculis flavescentibus.

Plura de hac avicula, quam plene describit character specificus, dicere supervacaneum habui, nisi quod species prius apud nos incognita, a Nova Hollandia nuperrime advenerit. De modo vivendi nihil est quod proferre possum; de hoc enim prorsus sileturs.

THE SPECKLED MANAKIN.

GENERIC CHARACTER.

Bill shorter than the head, somewhat triangular at the base, bent at the tip.
Feet gressorial.

SPECIFIC CHARACTER.

GREYISH-BROWN MANAKIN, undulated with dusky, the top of the head and the wings black speckled with white, the coverts of the tail red.

The supposed female is less vivid in colour, and the head is spotted with yellowish.

Of this bird, which is fully described by its specific character, it is unnecessary to say more than that it is a new species; having been lately received from New Holland, but unaccompanied by any particulars relative to its manner of life.

MEDUSA INFUNDIBULUM.

Character Genericus.

Corpus gelatinofum, orbiculatum (plerifque) de-depreffum.
Os fubtus centrale.

Character Specificus, &c.

MEDUSA OVATA, coftis ciliatis novem.
Gmel. Syft. Nat. p. 3152.

VOLVOX BEROE.
Lin. Syft. Nat. p. 1324.

In Infulæ Jamaicæ hiftoria formofam hanc Medufæ fpeciem primus notaffe videtur Dominus Browne; cujus defcriptionem cum lectoribus lubentiffime communicavi.

Forma eft ovata, obtufe actangula, cava, extremitate majore aperta, pellucida, fubftantia firma et gelata. Facillime fe contrahit et dilatat; inter natandum femper expanfa. Radii longitudinales validiores ad verticem, unde quafi a ftella pulchra et oblonga affurgunt, ad marginem fenfim attenuati. Singuli autem ferie tentaculorum gracilium breviumque ornantur, quæ hinc inde

inde ad arbitrium animalis a fummo ad imum celerrime moventur. Membrorum mollium et tenellorum quafi undatim fe invicem affequi properantium incitati curfus, variique et fole repercuffi colores nequeunt facile verbis exprimi. Circa infulas Jamaicæ occiduas frequenter fpectantur hæc animalia, raro tres pollices cum dimidio pollicis longitudine fuperantia, duofque vel duos cum dimidio in diametro.

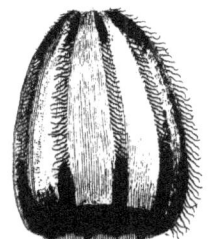

THE
FUNNEL MEDUSA.

GENERIC CHARACTER.

Body gelatinous, orbicular, in most species depressed.
Mouth beneath, central.

SPECIFIC CHARACTER.

OVATE MEDUSA with (commonly) nine ciliated ribs.

The elegant species of Medusa here represented, appears to have been first observed by Dr. Patrick Browne, who, in his History of Jamaica, has described it in the following words:

" This beautiful creature is of an oval form, obtusely octangular, hollow, open at the larger extremity, transparent, and of a firm gelatinous consistence. It contracts and widens with great facility, but is always open and expanded when it swims or moves. The longitudinal radii are strongest at the crown or smaller extremity, where they rise from a very beautiful oblong star, and diminish gradually from thence to the margin: but each of them is furnished with a single series of short, delicate, slender appendixes or limbs, that move

with

with great celerity either the one way or the other, as the creature pleafes to direct its flexions, and in a regular accelerated fucceffion from the top to the margin. It is impoffible to exprefs the livelinefs of the motions of thefe delicate organs, or the beautiful variety of colours that rife from them while they play to and fro in the rays of the fun; nor is it eafy to exprefs the fpeed and regularity with which the motions fucceed each other from one end of the rays to the other."

Thefe animals are frequently feen about the weftern iflands of Jamaica: they feldom exceed three inches and a half in length, or two and a half in the largeft tranfverfe diameter.

PAPILIO NESTOR.

****

CHARACTER GENERICUS.

Antennæ apicem verfus craffiores, fæpius clavato-capitatæ.
Alæ (fedentis) erectæ furfumque conniventes.
(*Volatu* diurno.)

Lin. Syſt. Nat. p. 744.

CHARACTER SPECIFICUS, &c.

PAPILIO alis dentatis fupra fufcis albo maculatis difcoque cæruleo, fubtus ocellis tribus quatuorque.

Fabr. Spec. Inf. 2. p. 24.

PAPILIO alis dentatis: fupra fufcis maculis difcoque cæruleis, fubtus ocellis tribus binifque.

Lin. Syſt. Nat. p. 752.
Eq. Achiv.

Papilionem Achillem in hoc opere jam defcriptum magnitudine fere æquat, forma eleganti fuperat Papilio Neſtor. Alarum oræ profunde denticulatæ funt, mediaque pars, feu difcus ex lucidiffime cæruleus; limbi

autem

autem funt nigri, maculis lunatis albis et cærulefcentibus, ut et figura demonftrat, notati. Americam Auftralem incolit papilio Neftor. Inferior fuperficies eft fufca, maculas habens ocellatas, marginibus centrifque albidis.

NESTOR.

Generic Character.

Antennæ or *Horns* thickening towards the upper part, and generally terminating in a knob, or club-shaped tip.
Wings (when sitting) erect, and meeting upwards. (*Flight* diurnal.)

Specific Character, &c.

BUTTERFLY with indented blackish wings with bright-blue disk and white spots; the under surface brown, with larger and smaller ocellated spots.

Mer. Sur. t. 9.
Cram. 2. t. 19. f. A. B.

The Papilio Nestor is nearly equal in size to the P: Achilles, which has already been figured in the present work; but is more elegant in shape, the wings being deeply indented or scolloped round the edges. The chief or middle part of all the wings is of the richest brilliant blue: the edges are black marked with lunated

lunated spots of white and blueish, as represented in the figure. It is a native of South America. The lower surface is brown, with some ocellated spots with whitish margins and centres.

MOTACILLA HIRUNDINACEA.

Character Genericus.

Rostrum subulatum, rectum: mandibulis subæqualibus.
Nares obovatæ.
Lingua lacero-emarginata.

Lin. Syst. Nat. p. 328.

Character Specificus.

MOTACILLA? chalybeo-nigra, gula pectore crissoque phoeniceis, abdomine niveo fascia longitudinali nigra.

Speciem hanc, Novæ Hollandiæ incolam, in Angliam non ita pridem illatam, ignorasse videntur ornithologi. Vultu est paululum ambiguo, et dubitari forsan possit an hirundini potius quam motacillæ sit similior. Cum vero prorsus sit impossibile avis penitus novæ (præsertim si ipsum specimen vel tantillum læsum sit) verum et certum locum in systemate designare; nomen igitur triviale dedi, quod admoneat ulterius quærendum esse, si detur aliquando occasio accuratius examinandi.

THE
SWALLOW WARBLER.

Generic Character.

Bill fubulated (or owl-fhaped;) ftrait; the mandibles nearly equal.
Noftrils nearly oval.
Tongue jagged, or lacerated towards the tip.

Specific Character.

BLACK WARBLER? with a glofs of fteel-blue, throat breaft and vent crimfon, abdomen white with a longitudinal band of black.

This is a fpecies hitherto unknown to ornithologifts: it is an inhabitant of New Holland, and was very lately brought into this kingdom. Its general appearance feems to be fomewhat doubtful, and it may be thought perhaps to make as near an approach to the genus Hirundo as to that of Motacilla. As it is impoffible, however, in new fpecies, efpecially when the fpecimens have received the fmalleft injury, to afcertain with perfect precifion their true place in fyftem, I have therefore

therefore applied to this bird a trivial name which may ferve as a hint for farther inquiry, fhould opportunity offer, of examining the fpecies in a more accurate manner.

GRYLLUS LAURIFOLIUS.

CHARACTER GENERICUS.

Caput inflexum, maxillosum, palpis instructum.
Antennæ setaceæ, seu filiformes.
Alæ quatuor, deflexæ, convolutæ: inferiores plicatæ.
Pedes postici saltatorii. *Ungues* ubique bini.

Lin. Syst. Nat. p. 693.

CHARACTER SPECIFICUS, &c.

GRYLLUS thorace subtetragono lævi trilobo, alis lanceolatis elytro obtusiore longioribus.

Lin. Syst. Nat. p. 695.

LOCUSTA thorace tetragono lævi, alis lanceolatis elytro longioribus.

Fab. spec. ins. 1. p. 356.

LOCUSTA maxima viridis, alis latissimis.

Sloan. jam. 2. p. 201. t. 236. f. 1.

Nomen inde adeptum est hoc insectum quod alarum thecæ seu elytra Lauri foliis simillima sint. In generibus Grylli et Mantis multis speciebus facies est quasi foliata;

foliata; quod voluiffe quodammodo videtur Natura, ut in arborum coma verfantes ab avium aliorumque hoftium rapacitate fiant fecuriores. Reperitur hæc grylli fpecies in America.

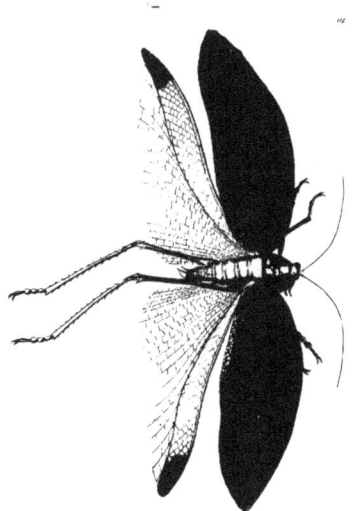

THE
BAY-LEAVED LOCUST.

GENERIC CHARACTER.

Head inflected, armed with jaws, and furnished with palpi or feelers.
Antennæ either setaceous or filiform.
Wings four, deflected, convolute; the inferior ones plaited.
Hind-feet formed for leaping. Claws on all the feet double.

SPECIFIC CHARACTER, &c.

LOCUST with smooth and somewhat tetragonal thorax, and wings (commonly) rather longer than the wing-sheaths.

THE BAY-LEAVED LOCUST.

This insect has obtained its name from the strong general resemblance which the upper or outer wings bear to the leaves of the Bay tree. Several species in the genera of Gryllus and Mantis are highly remarkable for this leaf-like appearance, which seems intended in some measure as a security to the animals
from

from the attacks of birds and other creatures while feated amongſt the foliage of the trees which they frequent. This ſpecies is a native of many parts of America.

TRIGLA CATAPHRACTA.

CHARACTER GENERICUS.

Caput loricatum lineis fcabris.
Membr: branch: radiis feptem.
Digiti liberi ante pinnas pectorales.

CHARACTER SPECIFICUS, &c.

TRIGLA digitis geminis, roftro furcato elongato, corpore octagono.
Lin. Syft. Nat. p. 496.

TRIGLA cirris plurimis, corpore octagono.
Art. gen. 46. *fyn.* 75.

Pifcium loricatorum feu *cataphractorum*, ut dicuntur, vix elegantior eft fpecies quam quæ in tabula depingitur. Unica eft e Triglis quæ hoc tegmine defenditur, cum reliquis omnibus hactenus cognitis fquamæ parvulæ obductæ fint. Caput mire conformatum: roftrum enim late bifurcum, apicibus obtufis; quod vel folum hunc pifcem fatis diftinguat a Cotto cataphracto aliifque nonnullis, cum quibus fortaffe eum fpectator incuri-

incuriofus, notifque quæ genus difcriminant parum
verfatus, poffet confundere. Color albido-fufco-pallet.
Longa eft, ut plurimum, Trigla cataphracta circiter
fex uncias. In mari nafcitur Mediterraneo.

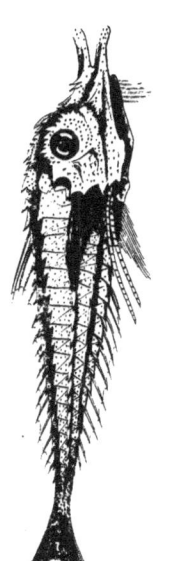

THE
MAILED GURNARD.

GENERIC CHARACTER.

Head covered with long plates.
Branchiostegous membrane with seven rays.
Appendages situated before the pectoral fins.

SPECIFIC CHARACTER, &c.

GURNARD with two pectoral appendages, elongated forked snout, and mailed body.

THE MAILED GURNARD.

Amongst the mailed or cataphracted fish, the species here represented is one of the most elegant. It is the only species of Trigla which is distinguished by this peculiar kind of coating; all the others yet known being covered with small scales. The form of the head is singular; the snout or upper jaw being widely bifurcated, with the divisions or processes obtuse. This forked appearance of the head is alone sufficient to distinguish this fish from the Cottus cataphractus and some others, with which an incurious spectator, not attending

ing to its generic characters, might perhaps be in danger of confounding it. Its colour is a very pale whitish brown, and its usual length about six inches. It is a native of the Mediterranean sea.

CRAX ALECTOR.

CHARACTER GENERICUS.

Rostrum basi cera obductum in utraque mandibula.
Pennæ caput tegentes revolutæ.
Lin. Syst. Nat. p. 269.

CHARACTER SPECIFICUS, &c.

CRAX cera flava, corpore nigro, ventre albo.
Lin. Syst. Nat. p. 269.

GALLUS INDICUS.
Sloan. Jam. 2. p. 302. t. 260.

MITUPORANGA.
Raii. Syn. p. 52. 6.

Crax Alector e maximis est gallinacei generis. In America Australi abundat, caroque ejus in deliciis habetur. Fit cicur nullo fere negotio. Coloribus nonnunquam variat. Femina fusco-ferruginea est.

THE COMMON CURASSOW.

Generic Character.

Bill on both mandibles covered with a cere.
Feathers on the head revolute.

Specific Character, &c.

BLACK CURASSOW with yellow cere; the lower part of the abdomen white.

LE HOCCO DE LA GUIANE.
Briss. orn. 1. p. 298. pl. 29.

MITUPORANGA.
Will. orn. p. 161. pl. 28.

The Crax Alector or black Curassow is one of the largest of the gallinaceous tribe. It is common in South America, where it is much esteemed as an article of food. It is easily domesticated, and is sometimes subject to vary in colour. The female is of a ferruginous brown.

MADREPORA CEREBRUM.

CHARACTER GENERICUS.

Animal Medusa.
Corallium cavitatibus lamelloso-stellatis.

Lin. Syst. Nat. p. 1272.

CHARACTER SPECIFICUS, &c.

MADREPORA subglobosa, anfractibus longissimis tortuosis, prominentiis plano-obtusis.

MADREPORA composita, labyrinthiformis hemisphærica, lamellis duplicato ordine integris obtusis, sinubus æqualibus.

Hort. Cliff. 489.

MADREPORA MEANDRITES.

Pall. el. zooph. p. 292. n. 171.

CORALLIUM CEREBRI FACIE.

Petiv. gaz. t. 68. n. 11.

Varia est hujus Madreporæ magnitudo. Interdum paucas tantum uncias, interdum duos pedes diametro superat. Forma illi est fere sphærica, perfectior tamen in certis speciminibus. Ob similitudinem quam habet superficies

superficies parti externæ corticatæ seu cinericiæ (ut vocatur) in quadrupedum cerebro, nomen illi inde commune *Lapis cerebri* inditum est. Alia est species, huic de qua jam loquimur simillima, quamque primo visu eandem putares; et sane dubitari possit sitne hujus varietas; differt enim tantum in gyris prominentibus, qui compressiores et acutiores, non complanati. Notandum est Madreporis rotundatis non raro inesse duo vel tria foramina, diametri non exiguæ, ad cylindros in ipso corallio terebratos ducentia. Non videntur hujusmodi foramina naturæ opus esse, sed aliorum animalium, Terebellarum nempe (ut vocantur) quæ corallium perforant, interdumque in imis hisce tubis quasi in cubile jacentes reperiuntur.

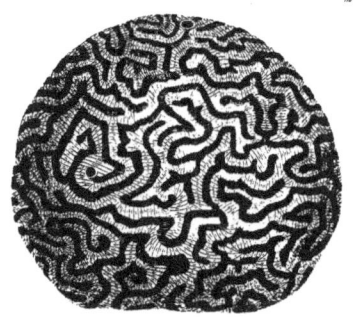

THE
BRAIN MADREPORE.

GENERIC CHARACTER.

Animal resembling a Medusa.
Coral marked with lamellar striated cavities.

SPECIFIC CHARACTER, &c.

NEARLY GLOBULAR MADREPORE, with very long tortuous undulations, the prominent ones terminating flattish.

THE GREAT BRAIN-STONE.

The Madrepore represented on this plate is found of various sizes, from a few inches to upwards of two feet in diameter. Its form is nearly globular, but much more accurately so in some specimens than in others. From the general resemblance which the undulated surface bears to the cortical or exterior part of the brain in quadrupeds, it has obtained its common title of Brain-stone. There is another species which in size and general appearance so very nearly resembles the present, that on a cursory view it would readily pass for the same; and indeed can scarce be regarded in any
other

other light than that of a variety. The difference confifts in the prominent undulations, which in that fpecies are of a more compreffed form, fo as to rife with a fharp edge; not flattened as in the prefent fpecies. I fhould obferve that in the globular Madrepores are often, and indeed generally, feen one or two or more round orifices of confiderable diameter, and which lead to cylindrical perforations in the body of the coral. Thefe holes do not feem fo much owing to the natural ftructure of the Madrepore itfelf, as to the operation of other animals, fuch as Terebellæ, which are fometimes found imbedded in thefe tubes.

MANTIS SICCIFOLIA.

CHARACTER GENERICUS.

Caput nutans maxillosum, palpis instructum.
Antennæ (plerisque) setaceæ.
Alæ quatuor, membranaceæ, (plerisque) convolutæ; inferiores plicatæ.
Pedes antici compressi, subtus serrato-denticulati, armati ungue solitario et digito setaceo laterali articulato. *Postici* quatuor læves, gressorii.
Thorax linearis, elongatus, angustatus.

Lin. Syst. Nat. p. 689.

CHARACTER SPECIFICUS, &c.

MANTIS thorace denticulato, femoribus ovatis membranaceis.

Lin. Syst. Nat. p. 689.
Roes. ins. 2. t. 17. fig. 45.
Edw. av. t. 258.

Omnibus Mantin hanc obiter intuentibus, præcipue si alarum thecæ seu elytra claudantur, in mentem venit folii mortui exsiccatique similitudo. Verisimile est vivæ virescere potius colores quam subfuscari: quæ tamen in Europam illata sunt specimina respondent tabulæ. Cum ei alarum inferiorum rudimenta tantum sint, non impossibile est quin revera sit larva speciei cujusdam hactenus non plene cognitæ et descriptæ; ni potius e numero sit illorum infectorum quæ constanti naturæ consilio alis carent, quorum multa sunt non solum in classe *Hemiptera* sed et *Coleoptera*; in certis scilicet *Cimicis*, *Carabi*, aliorumque speciebus.

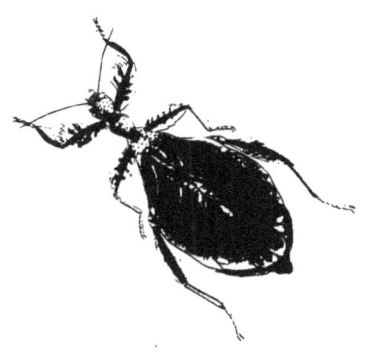

THE
DRY LEAF MANTIS.

GENERIC CHARACTER.

Head unsteady; Mouth armed with jaws, and furnished with palpi.
Antennæ setaceous, (some few species excepted.)
Wings four, membranaceous, in most species convoluted: the lower ones (generally) plicated.
Feet anterior compressed, serrated beneath, armed with a lateral solitary claw and jointed process; *posterior* four smooth, formed for walking.
Thorax (in most species) elongated and narrowed.

SPECIFIC CHARACTER, &c.

MANTIS with denticulated thorax and ovate membranaceous thighs.

THE WALKING LEAF.

Edw. pl. 258.

The very remarkable shape and colour of this insect uniformly suggest the idea of a dried or withered leaf, which the animal, when its wings are closed, so much

much resembles, that, on a cursory view, it might easily be mistaken for such. It is not improbable that in a recent state the colour may be rather green than brownish: the specimens however which are brought into Europe are generally of the tinge represented in the plate. It is remarkable that this curious animal has merely the rudiments of under or lower wings. It is therefore not improbable that it may in reality be the larva of some species not yet fully described; or else that it is a species which is naturally apterous; a circumstance of which several instances occur, not only in the class *Hemiptera*, but also in that of *Coleoptera*; as is sufficiently proved in some species of *Cimex*, *Carabus*, and others.

TANTALUS RUBER.

Character Genericus.
Rostrum longum, subulatum, teretiusculum, subarcuatum.
Facies ultra oculos nuda.
Lingua brevis, lata.
Saccus jugularis nudus.
Nares ovatæ.
Pedes tetradactyli, basi palmati.
Lin. Syst. Nat. p. 240.

Character Specificus, &c.
TANTALUS facie rostro pedibusque rubris, corpore sanguineo, alarum apicibus nigris.
Lin. Syst. Nat. p. 241.
NUMENIUS brasiliensis coccineus.
Briss. av. 5. p. 344. t. 29. f. 1. 2.
NUMENIUS RUBER.
Catesb. Car. 1. p. 84. t. 84.
NUMENIUS INDICUS.
Clus. exot. 366.

Avium nitidissimarum parens orbis occiduus paucas alit hac splendidiores, cui totus vestitus, exceptis remigum longiorum apicibus, lætissime est coccineus. Rostrum

trum pedesque pallentes rubent. Varias licet Americæ partes incolat, in auftralioribus tamen frequentior eft, Magnitudine Numenio communi fere æqualis eft, eodemque propemodum utitur vivendi modo.

THE SCARLET IBIS.

GENERIC CHARACTER.

Bill long, thick at the base, incurvated.
Face, and sometimes the whole head, naked.
Nostrils linear.
Tongue short.
Toes connected at the base by a membrane.

Lath. Syn. 3. p. 104.

SPECIFIC CHARACTER, &c.

SCARLET IBIS with red beak and legs; the wings tipped with black.

SCARLET IBIS.
Lath. Synops. 3. p. 106.
RED CURLEW.
Catesb. Car. 1. p. 84. pl. 84.

Amongst the brilliant birds of the western Continent few are more conspicuous than the present; the whole plumage of which, except the tips of the wings, is of the brightest and most vivid scarlet. The bill and legs are of a pale red. It is found in many parts of America, but is most common in the southern provinces. Its size is nearly that of a Curlew, which it also resembles in its manner of life.

GORDIUS AQUATICUS.

CHARACTER GENERICUS.

Corpus filiforme, æquale, læve.
Lin. Syst. Nat. p. 1075.

CHARACTER SPECIFICUS, &c.

GORDIUS pallidus extremitatibus nigris.
Lin. Syst. Nat. p. 1075.

SETA, s. vitulus aquaticus.
Aldr. inf. 720. t. 765.

GORDIUS SETA.
Müll. hist. verm. 1. 2. p. 30. n. 161.

SETA PALUSTRIS.
Planc. conch. app. c. 22. t. 5. f. F.

Vermis iste, setæ simillimus, qui Gordius vocatur, in aquis mollibus et stagnantibus præcipue cernitur, idque fere omni tempore, frequentius autem æstivo. Longus, ut plurimum, vix quatuor uncias, pertingit interdum ad quinque vel etiam sex. Color communis fusco-pallet, extremitatibus nigricantibus, vel saltem magis infuscatis reliquo corpore. Nomen Gordii, quod et generi commune, inde adeptus est, quia contorquere se et colligere soleat

soleat quasi in nodum qui *Gordius* nuncupatur. Cum diu manserit convolutus, iterum in pristinam longitudinem gradatim se explicat. Interdum in aquis movetur more hirudinis, satis celeriter; alias cunctanter, gressuque quo nihil concipi potest languidius. Nomen vulgare *Hair-worm*, non ob formam solummodo datum est; sed quod eum revera ortum esse a seta quæ ab equo seu alio animali in aquas deciderat, olim crediderit indoctum vulgus, etiamnum erroris tenax. Si Gordius digitum morsu læserit, paronychiam non raro excitare dicitur: idque in Suecia subinde accidere a Linnæo memoratur fide non modo rusticorum, sed experimento viri eruditi, naturæ et veritatis studiosissimi. Possum quoque egomet testimonium proferre hominis fide dignissimi, qui mihi retulit, Gordium, quem incaute nuda manu ex aquis eripuit, extremum sibi digitum vulnerasse, indeque exortam esse paronychiam. An insit morsui peculiaris quædam irritatio, an ab alia qualibet punctura idem proveniret effectus, vix ausim dicere. Piaculum foret, si de Gordio locutus morbum nomine *Venæ Medinensis* cognitum silerem, qui oritur a Gordii specie quæ in calidioribus mundi regionibus (cum adhuc forte parvula sit) sub cutim irrepere dicitur, ibique in magnam crescere longitudinem, et difficillime extrahi, dolorem summum molestiamque excitans. Nec prætereundum est, gordii speciem, (ipsum fortasse vulgarem dum adhuc junior) in animalibus variis præter omnem expectationem inveniri; in scarabæis scilicet, erucis, aliisque insectis. Immo memini meipsum in cerebro Lacertæ aquaticæ Linnæi Gordios adeo exiguos observasse, ut cum microscopio acurate eos examinassem, unciæ millesimam partem vix superare viderentur.

Vitæ

Vitæ tenacissimus est Gordius vulgaris, et quamvis in aqua servatus quasi mortuus multas horas jaceat, postea tamen integrari videntur pristinæ vires. Notandum est reperiri eum non modo in aqua sed interdum in ipsa terra; in hortis præcipue post pluviam, et in humo argillacea, in qua facillime et liberrime se movere solet.

THE COMMON GORDIUS,
OR
HAIR-WORM.

Generic Character.

Body filiform, equal, smooth.

Specific Character, &c.

PALE-BROWN GORDIUS with dark extremities.

THE COMMON HAIR-WORM.

The Gordius aquaticus or common Hair-Worm is principally an inhabitant of soft stagnant waters, and may be found during the greatest part of the year, but is most plentiful in the summer months. It grows to the length of five or six inches, but is not very often seen of more than about four inches. Its most general colour is a palish brown, with the extremities blackish, or at least darker than the other parts. It has obtained the generic name of Gordius, from its having a habit of sometimes twisting itself into such peculiar contorsions as to resemble a complicated or Gordian knot. In this state it often continues for a considerable space; and

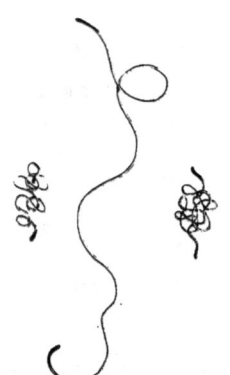

and then flowly difengages itfelf, and extends its body at full length. Sometimes it moves in the water with a pretty quick undulating motion like that of a leech; and at other times in the floweft and moft languid manner imaginable. Its popular name of Hair-Worm was not given it from its form alone, but from an idea that it was produced from the hair of horfes and other animals which had been caft in the water: an opinion which is not even yet extinct amongft the vulgar. A remarkable circumftance relative to this animal is, that its bite, which it fometimes inflicts on being taken out of the water, has been known to produce the complaint called a whitlow. This is mentioned by Linnæus as a popular idea in Sweden, and which had been confirmed by the experience of a perfon of high reputation. I can alfo add the teftimony of a gentleman of great veracity, who affured me that on having incautioufly taken a Gordius out of the water, he was bit by it on the tip of his finger, and that in confequence of the bite a whitlow foon took place. Whether however there be really any thing peculiarly irritating in the bite of this worm, or whether a fimilar puncture caufed by any other means might not produce the fame effect, I cannot take upon me to determine.

It would be unpardonable on this fubject to omit obferving that the complaint called the Guinea-Worm, or Vena Medinenfis, which fometimes happens in the warmer regions, is owing to a fpecies of Gordius, which is faid to infinuate itfelf (probably when very fmall) under the fkin; where it grows to a great length; is productive of very troublefome fymptoms, and is extremely difficult to extract. It is remarkable alfo that a fpecies
of

of Gordius, perhaps the Gordius aquaticus in a very young ſtate, occurs not unfrequently in animals in which one would leaſt expect to find it; viz. in beetles of different ſorts, in caterpillars, and other inſects; and I once diſcovered in the brain of the ſmaller Water-Newt (Lacerta aquatica. Lin.) a number of microſcopic Gordii ſo extremely minute as not to exceed the thouſandth part of an inch in length. The gordius aquaticus is very tenacious of life, and after being kept a long time in a veſſel of water, will ſometimes appear perfectly motionleſs, and as if dead, for ſeveral hours; after which it will again aſſume its former vigour, and ſeem as healthy as at firſt. It ſhould alſo be obſerved that the Gordius is not unfrequently found in earth as well as in water; eſpecially in garden-ground after rain; and in clayey ſoils, in which it moves with great facility.

COLUBER CERASTES.

CHARACTER GENERICUS.

Scuta abdominalia.
Squamæ fubcaudales.

Lin. Syſt. Nat. p. 275.

CHARACTER SPECIFICUS, &c.

COLUBER cornutus fufco-ferrugineus, fcutis abdominalibus 150, fquamis fubcaudalibus 25.

Bellon. it. 203.
Ellis. act. angl. 56. t. 14.

Coluber Ceraſtes, longus ut plurimum, pedem feu quindecim uncias, cornubus duobus incurvis fupra oculos fitis et antrorfum fpectantibus infignis eſt: quæ licet nequaquam fimilia fint quadrupedum cornubus, nec vulnus poffint vel inferre vel defendere, augent tamen quodammodo odium quod contra totum genus ferpentinum plerique folemus concipere, ipfiufque animalis vultum maligniorem et truculentiorem reddunt. In Africa innafcitur Ceraſtes, præcipuamque fibi fedem delegit in defertis ficcis et arenofis. In Ægypto? communis eſt, nec non in certis Nubiæ et Abyffiniæ partibus. In Syria quoque et Arabia plurimus. Ad viperæ vulgaris

vulgaris fimilitudinem non parum accedit Ceraftes; ob morfum tamen magis eft pertimefcendus, quippe non folum eos qui incaute illum proculcant vulnerat, verum etiam magno et repentino impetu in prætereuntes e longinquo infilit. In multis Africæ regionibus, fi qua fides peregrinatoribus digniffimis, funt qui hos nec non alios venenatos ferpentes medicamentis pollentibus hebetatos poffunt fafcinare; quique rite parati nihil ab illis metuunt, omnigena licet provocatione irritentur. Lubenter crederem ferpentes ita delenitos, telis venenatis, dentibus fcilicet tubulatis prius fuiffe privatos, ni Brucio, cui in itineribus Africanis plurimæ oblatæ funt occafiones veritatem eruendi, longe alia mens effet.
" Audacter poffum affirmare me in urbe Cairo vidiffe
" (quod fane alicui in quotidianum datur confpectum,)
" errantem quendam ab avium conditarum coemeteriis,
" qui nudis manibus Ceraftem e plurimis in imo dolio
" jacentibus fublatum capiti impofuit, pileoque com-
" muni rubro cooperuit; poftea in pectore fovit, et
" quafi monile circa collum ligavit. Simul ac vero
" gallinæ admoveretur ipfiffimus hic ferpens, momordit
" eam, illaque cito periit. Tandem homo, ut faftigi-
" um operi imponeret, ferpentem collo prehenfum, a
" cauda incipiens ftatim abfque ullo faftidii figno, ac
" fi quis daucum aut *celeri* devoravit."

Addit Brucius omnes populos nigros in regno *Sennaar* perfecte hoc modo contra Ceraftes armari, eofque non folum in pectoribus imponere, fed cum iis ludere, et in fefe timoris et periculi expertes invicem conjicere, uti pueri poma.

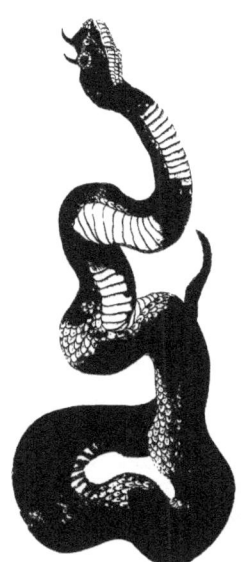

THE
CERASTES,
OR
HORNED VIPER.

GENERIC CHARACTER.

Tranfverfe *Lamellæ* under the abdomen.
Alternate *Scales* under the tail.

SPECIFIC CHARACTER, &c.

FERRUGINOUS-BROWN HORNED VIPER
with about 150 abdominal plates and 25 fub-
caudal fcales.

THE CERASTES, OR HORNED SNAKE.

The Coluber Ceraftes, which commonly grows to the length of about a foot or fifteen inches, is diftinguifhed by a pair of horns or curved proceffes, feated above the eyes and pointing forwards. Thefe horns have nothing analogous in their ftructure to the horns of quadrupeds, and are by no means to be confidered in the light of either offenfive or defenfive weapons: they increafe however the natural antipathy fo generally felt againft the ferpent tribe, and give the animal a more

than

than ordinary appearance of malignity. This serpent is a native of Africa, and is principally found in sandy deserts and dry places. In Egypt? it is common, as well as in some particular parts of Nubia and Abyssinia. It also abounds in Syria and Arabia. It bears a very great analogy to the common viper: its bite is perhaps still more to be dreaded, since exclusive of the general danger in treading accidentally on one of these reptiles, and thus irritating it unawares, it possesses a propensity of springing with great suddenness to a considerable distance, and assailing without provocation those who happen to approach it. In many parts of Africa, according to the testimony of the most respectable travellers, there prevails a method of charming, as it were, or stupifying these, as well as other poisonous serpents, by the use of certain preparations of such powerful efficacy as effectually to secure the person so prepared from being in the least bitten by the animals, though oppressed by every species of irritation. A suspicion might naturally arise that the serpents thus treated had been first deprived of their fangs, and consequently of their power of poisoning; but that this is not the case, is expressly declared by Mr. Bruce, who, during his African travels, had ample opportunities of witnessing these extraordinary experiments. On this subject Mr. Bruce expresses himself as follows:

" I will not hesitate to aver, that I have seen at Cairo
" (and this may be seen daily, without trouble or ex-
" pence) a man who came from above the catacombs
" where the mummy-birds are kept, who has taken a
" Cerastes with his naked hand from a number of
" others lying at the bottom of the tub; has put it
" upon

" upon his bare head, covered it with the common red
" cap he wears, then taken it out, put it in his breaſt,
" and tied it about his neck like a necklace; after
" which it has been applied to a hen, and bit it, which
" has died in a few minutes: and to complete the ex-
" periment, the man has taken it by the neck, and
" beginning at his tail, has ate it, as one would do a
" carrot, or a ſtock of celery, without any ſeeming
" repugnance."

Mr. Bruce adds, that all the black people in the kingdom of Sennaar are perfectly armed in this manner againſt the bite of the Ceraſtes, and put them at any time into their boſoms, and throw them at one another as children do apples, with the moſt perfect impunity,

DIDUS INEPTUS.

Character Genericus.

Rostrum medio coarctatum rugis duabus tranfverfis: utraque mandibula inflexo apice.
Facies ultra oculos nuda.
Lin. Syst. Nat. p. 267.

Character Specificus, &c.

DIDUS nigricans albido-nebulofus, pedibus tetradactylis.
DIDUS INEPTUS.
Lin. Syst. Nat. p. 267.
GALLUS gallinaceus peregrinus.
Clus. exot. 99. t. 100.
CYGNUS CUCULLATUS.
Nieremb. nat. 231.
STRUTHIO CUCULLATUS.
Lin. Syst. Nat. X. p. 155.

Si unico vero et genuino exemplari, quod ab ipfa vita delineari dicitur, undeque reliqua fere omnia adumbrata funt, danda fit fides; hebetat vultum hujus avis tam plumbea ftupiditas, ut nomen inde triviale adepta fit.

fit. Mole faltem æqualis effe dicitur cygno; cujus ab eleganti forma in reliquis longe abhorret. Color generalis niger eft; alarum autem pars media, abdomen, et in cauda plumæ aliquot fere albent. Roftri enormis maxilla fuperior prope apicem macula magna rubente diftinguitur, bafi feu lata parte longe fuper frontem retro excurrente, ut facies quafi cucullata videatur. Mirum eft, cum fcientiæ naturalis ftudio quotidianum fere nunc dierum fiat incrementum, deeffe vel unicum fpecimen fingularis iftius avis, quæ, quantum ipfe comperi, rariffime in Europam illata eft ab anno 1598, quo tempore a parvula Mauritii infula Indica adveniffe dicitur. Defcripferunt eam plurimi auctores, Nierembergius fcilicet, Bontius, Clufiufque inter vetuftiores, et e recentioribus Buffonus, Edwardus, Briffonus, aliique. Pene tamen ignofceremus dubitantibus an revera extiterit, ni aliter teftarentur Herbertus aliique qui fe ipfam in natalibus regionibus fuis oculis confpexiffe profitentur; ipfeque Willoughbeius fuum calculum adderet, qui afferit fe fpolia ejus in mufeo Joannis Tradefcantii vidiffe. In Mufeo Britannico affervatur, quod plurimi auctores imitati funt, ipfum unde avis depicta eft archetypum. Frumento vefci dicitur Didus, et ingenio effe manfueto. Sitne ad edendum utilis varie difputatur. Alii durum et injucundum ducunt; alii contra dignum putant ut menfæ apponatur; pectus præcipue, quod, tefte Bontio, tantum eft, ut horum tria quatuorve centum convivis fufficiant. Africæ et Indiæ Orientalis infulas inhabitat.

Denique, liceat fortaffe nobis conjicere annon *Diomedeæ exulantis* Linnæi nondum ætate provectæ infidæ delineationi Didus originem debeat. Quod fi concedatur, certe

certe manus pictoris nimium nimiumque oblita eſt veritatis, quæ pedes Diomedeæ pinnatos alaſque ampliſſimas et longiſſimas neglexerit, ut taceam cætera, in quibus hæ aves nullo modo convenire queant. E contrario tamen negari non poſſit roſtrum Diomedeæ roſtro quod Didi putatur non multum eſſe diſſimile; et ſi ſpecimen Diomedeæ junioris examinemus cui color adhuc imperfectus, cujuſque ſuper alas cæteraſque partes albedo cum nigredine commiſcetur, præſertim ſi avem torpidam et ſubſidentem fingimus, quod interdum fit, non omnino impoſſibile fatebimur quin a falſa aliqua hujuſmodi repræſentatione Didus originem duxerit. Charltonus in libro cui titulus *Onomaſticon Zoicon*, aſſerit roſtrum cum capite Didi tunc temporis in Muſeo Regalis Societatis Londinenſis fuiſſe ſervatum. Quod tamen ille roſtrum Didi cenſuit nihil aliud fortaſſe fuerit quam Diomedeæ roſtrum. Res igitur non prorſus caret dubio, et optandum admodum eſt ut avis ipſa vera et genuina, ſi modo talis alicubi exſtet, laudabili phyſicorum hodiernorum diligentia in Europam tandem aſportetur.

THE DODO.

Generic Character.

Bill large, bending inward in the middle of the upper mandible, marked with two oblique ribs, and much hooked at the end.
Nostrils placed obliquely near the edge, in the middle of the bill.
Legs short, thick, feathered a little below the knees.
Toes three forward, one backward.

Pennant.

Specific Character, &c.

BLACKISH DODO, clouded with whitish; with tetradactylous feet.

THE DODO.
Will. orn. p. 153. pl. 27.
Edw. pl. 294.

DOD-EERSEN, or VALGH-VOGEL.
Herbert. trav. p. 382. pl. in p. 383.

This bird, if we may depend on the fidelity of the only original figure, (which is said to have been taken from the life, and from which almost all authors have hitherto

hitherto copied,) is distinguished by an aspect of such confirmed stupidity, as to have obtained the trivial name of *ineptus*. In size it is said at least to equal, if not exceed, a swan, but in shape and general appearance forms a striking contrast to that elegant bird. Its prevailing colour is black, but the middle of the wings, the belly, and some of the tail feathers are white, or nearly so. The beak, which is of a very singular form, and of enormous size, is distinguished near the tip by a large red patch on the upper part; while the base or broad part runs far back over the front, so as to give the face a sort of hooded appearance. It is astonishing that in the present improved state of natural history, we should still be at a loss for a single specimen of this extraordinary bird, which, so far as I am able to discover, has scarce been imported into Europe since the year 1598, nearly at which period it is said to have been brought from the little island of Mauritius in the East Indies. It has been described by several authors, as Nieremberg, Bontius, and Clusius, amongst the older writers, and by the Count de Buffon, Edwards, Brisson, and others amongst the moderns. Were it not, however, for the attestations of Herbert and others, who profess to have seen it in its native regions, together with that of Mr. Willoughby, who assures us that he saw a skin of it in the Museum of Sir John Tradescant, we might be almost inclined to call in question the existence of so singular an animal. The original figure above mentioned, and which has been repeated by so many authors, is preserved in the British Museum. This bird is said to be granivorous and of a gentle nature. With respect to its merit as an article of food,

the

the opinion of authors seems to vary; some representing it as tough and unpleasant, while others consider it as by no means ill adapted for the table; especially the breast, which, according to Bontius, is of such a size that three or four of them are enough for a very large company. It is an inhabitant of Africa and the East-Indian islands.

After all, can it be possible that an Albatross, (Diomedea exulans Lin.) not fully grown, and inaccurately represented by a draughtsman, may have given rise to the supposed existence of the Dodo? If this be granted, we must surely admit an uncommon degree of carelessness in the painter, who could thus neglect to express the webs on the feet of the Albatross, as well as to represent the wings extremely large and long, instead of small and short; together with other particulars in which the two birds can by no means be made to agree. Yet, on the other hand, it is undeniable that the general appearance of the beak of an Albatross is not greatly dissimilar to that of the supposed Dodo. And if we contemplate a young or half-grown specimen of the great Albatross, before it has arrived at its proper colour, and while there is a mixture of black and white on the wings and other parts, and to this superadd the heavy and crouching posture in which it sometimes appears, it will perhaps seem not absolutely impossible that an erroneous sketch from such a bird may have been the basis on which the existence of the Dodo has hitherto stood. Charleton in his *Onomasticon Zoicon*, affirms that the bill and head of the Dodo were then in the Museum of the Royal Society. This reputed bill of a Dodo may however have been

nothing

nothing more than that of an Albatrofs. The fubject therefore may be ftill confidered as in fome degree doubtful, and it remains to wifh that the laudable zeal and fpirited exertions of modern naturalifts may at length put an end to the uncertainty by importing the real bird into Europe, if it can be found to exift.

PENNATULA ARGENTEA.

CHARACTER GENERICUS.

Flores Hydræ, ad marginem denticulatum pinnarum.
Stirps libera, fubulata, apice pinnata.
Lin. Syft. Nat. p. 1321.

CHARACTER SPECIFICUS, &c.

PENNATULA penniformis lanceolata, ftirpe lævi tereti, pinnis creberrimis imbricatis.

PENNATULA lanceolata pennæ facie, ftirpe lævi tereti, pinnis creberrimis imbricatis dentatis virgatis.
Soland. et Ellis zooph. p. 67. n. 10.

Inter maximas quæ hactenus notæ funt Pennatulas habenda eft hæc fpecies, nulli cedens pulchritudine: eft enim argenteo-alba, utrinque fuper partes expanfas feu penniformes lineis aterrimis eleganter ftriata. Rariffima eft, et maria incolit Indica. Delineata eft figura magnitudine naturali ab eximio fpecimine quod fuppeditavit Mufeum Britannicum.

THE
SILVER SEA-PEN.

Generic Character.

Animal free, or locomotive.
Body (generally) expanding into processes on the upper part.
Processes or branches furnished with rows of tubular denticles.
Polype-head proceeding from each tube.

Specific Character, &c.

LANCEOLATE FEATHER-SHAPED PEN-NATULA, with round smooth stem and thick-set imbricated pinnules.

SILVER SEA-PEN.
Ellis. and Soland: zooph. p. 66. t. 8. f. 1. 2. 3.

Of all the Pennatulæ yet known the present is one of the largest as well as the most specious in its appearance; being of a beautiful silvery white, elegantly striated on each of the feather-like processes with lines or
streaks

ftreaks of the deepeft black. It is extremely rare, and is a native of the Indian feas. The figure here given is copied from the very fine fpecimen in the Britifh Mufeum, and reprefents the animal in its natural fize.

PAPILIO RIPHEUS.

CHARACTER GENERICUS.

Antennæ apicem verfus craffiores, fæpius clavato-capitatæ.

Alæ fedentis erectæ furfumque conniventes (volatu diurno.)

Lin. Syſt. Nat. p. 744.

CHARACTER SPECIFICUS, &c.

PAPILIO alis fexdentato-caudatis nigris viridi fafciatis, pofterioribus medio aureo-rubris nigro maculatis.

PALILIO alis fexdentato-caudatis nigris viridi fafciatis, pofterioribus fubtus macula ani ferruginea nigro punctata.

Gmel. Syſt. Nat. p. 2235.
Fabr. mant. inſ. 2. p. 6. n. 43.
Cram. pap. 33. t. 385. f. A. B.

Eq. Achiv.

Papilionem in hac tabula depinximus non modo rariffimum, fed etiam coloribus fplendiffimis omnibus fere fui generis antecellentem. Haud multis abhinc annis in Europa innotuit hæc fpecies in perpaucis mufeis vel nunc

nunc conspicienda. Indiæ Orientalis est incola, et in China præcipue invenitur. Papilioni Leilo Linnæi valde affinis est tum forma tum coloribus; jactat tamen majorem elegantiam lautioremque varietatem. Eruca, hujus papilionis parens adhuc incognita est, verisimile autem est eam erucæ papilionis Leili a Domina Merian inter insecta Surinamensia depictæ non absimilem esse.

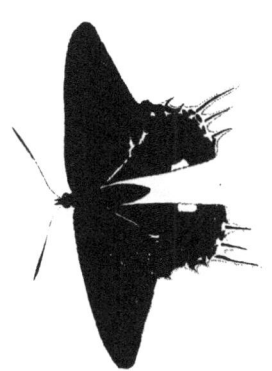

RIPHEUS,
OR THE
ORIENTAL EMPEROR.

Generic Character.

The *Antennæ* or *Horns* thickening towards the upper part, and generally terminating in a knob, or club-shaped tip.
The *Wings* (when sitting) erect, and meeting upwards. (*Flight* diurnal.)

Specific Character.

BLACK BUTTERFLY fasciated with golden-green; the lower wings marked in the middle with a large patch of golden-red spotted with black, and furnished with six elongated or subcaudated processes.

Cram. pap. 38. t. 385. f. A. B.
Drury. 2. pl. 23. f. 1. 2. ?

We have here represented a Papilio, which, exclusive of the extreme rarity of the species, may perhaps be pronounced the most beautiful of that splendid tribe. It is but a few years since this gay insect became known in Europe, and it is at present so rare as to be found in

very

very few collections. It is an East-Indian insect, but is principally found in China. It is very nearly allied both in shape and general disposition of colours to the Papilio Leilus; but is still more elegant, and displays a much richer variety of tints. The caterpillar of this butterfly is yet unknown; but it probably bears a near resemblance to that of Papilio Leilus, which has been figured amongst the Surinam insects by Madam Merian.

PICUS ERYTHROCEPHALUS.

CHARACTER GENERICUS.

Rostrum polyedrum, rectum : apice cuneato.
Nares pennis setaceis recumbentibus obtectae.
Lingua teres, lumbriciformis, longissima, mucronata, apice retrorsum aculeata setis.
Pedes scansorii.

Lin. Syst. Nat. p. 173.

CHARACTER SPECIFICUS, &c.

PICUS capite toto rubro, alis caudaque nigris, abdomine albo.

Lin. Syst. Nat. p. 174.

PICUS ERYTHROCEPHALUS VIRGINIENSIS.

Briss. av. 4. p. 53. n. 19. t. 3. f. 1.

Notissima est haec pici species per omnem fere Septentrionalem Americam, habeturque arvis et pomariis inimicissima, zeaeque et fructibus magnam stragem inferre. Elegans est, si quae alia, et concinna. Caput collumque laetissime phoenicea. Caetera avis nigrat quasi polita non sine nitore quodam caeruleo ; si excipias pectus, abdomen, uropygium, remigesque secundarios,

cundarios, quæ omnia nivea funt, fcapis eorundem remigum nigris. Roftrum pedefque faturatim plumbea. Mas et fœmina valde inter fe fimiles: fœminæ tamen caput minus rubet, immo interdum fere fufcum. Magnitudine prope æqualis eft hæc fpecies pico maculato majori Anglico, qui picus major Linnæi.

THE
RED-HEADED WOODPECKER.

GENERIC CHARACTER.

Bill angular, strait, cuneated at the tip.
Nostrils covered with reflected bristly feathers.
Tongue cylindric, worm-shaped, very long, sharp-pointed, and (generally) aculeated at the tip with reflex bristles.
Feet formed for climbing, viz. two toes forward and two backward.

SPECIFIC CHARACTER, &c.

BLACK WOODPECKER with the head and neck crimson; breast, abdomen, and shorter wing-feathers white.

RED-HEADED WOODPECKER.
Catesb. car. 1. pl. 20.

The species of Woodpecker here figured is extremely common in most parts of North America, and is considered as a most destructive enemy to plantations and orchards, devouring great quantities of maize and fruit. It is a bird of singular beauty and neatness of appearance. The head and neck are of the richest crimson: the rest of the bird of a deep polished black, with a blueish

blueish gloss, except the breast, belly, rump, and shorter feathers of the wings, which are snow-white. The shafts of the white wing-feathers are black. The beak and legs are of a deep lead-colour. The male and female greatly resemble each other, but the head of the female is less rich in colour, and sometimes even brownish. The size of this species is nearly that of the greater spotted English Woodpecker, or Picus Major of Linnæus.

RANA ARBOREA.

CHARACTER GENERICUS.

Corpus tetrapodum, nudum, ecaudatum.

Lin. Syst. Nat. p. 354.

CHARACTER SPECIFICUS, &c.

RANA corpore lævi: fubtus punctis contiguis tuberculato, pedibus fiffis, unguibus orbiculato-dilatatis.

Lin. Syst. Nat. p. 357.

RANUNCULUS VIRIDIS.

Gefn. pifc. 808.

RANA ARBOREA S. RANUNCULUS VIRIDIS.

Raj. quadr. 251.

In Anglia licet ignoretur bella hæc et parvula ranæ fpecies, Galliæ tamen, Germaniæ, multifque Europæis regionibus communis eft. Inter arborum folia præcipue verfatur, quorum, ut plurimum, paginæ inferiori folet adhærere; pedibus ad hoc ipfum mire formatis, cum fcilicet fingulus digitus in orbiculum depreffum definat; ita ut rana a glabra quavis fuperficie fatis fe-

cura

cura poffit pendere. Nafcitur, ut et reliquum genus, primo gyrinus: fœminæ enim, ut ova deponant, arbores deferunt, et aquas petunt; quo tempore mas faccum feu globum magnum e gula protrudit, alias vix et ne vix vifibilem.

THE
TREE FROG.

GENERIC CHARACTER.

Body four-footed, naked, tailed.

SPECIFIC CHARACTER, &c.

GREEN FROG, with unwebbed feet and orbicular flattened toes.

THE TREE FROG.

The beautiful little species of frog here represented is not uncommon in many parts of Europe, as France, Germany, &c. but is not found in England. It resides amongst the foliage of trees, and generally adheres to the under side of the leaves, the structure of the feet being finely adapted for this power; each toe terminating in an orbicular flattened process, by means of which the animal can apply itself with perfect security to the smoothest surface. Like others of its genus, it is first produced in the state of a tadpole; the females during the breeding season leaving the trees, and betaking themselves to the water, in order to deposit their spawn. The male during that period has a large inflated gular pouch or globe, which at other times is scarce ever visible.

ACARUS AURATUS.

CHARACTER GENERICUS.

Pedes octo.
Oculi duo ad latera capitis.
Tentacula duo articulata, pediformia.

Lin. Syst. Nat. p. 1022.

CHARACTER SPECIFICUS, &c.

ACARUS ORBICULATUS PLANIUSCULUS, aureo-maculatus, supra excavato-punctatus, abdomine subcrenato.

ACARUS IGUANÆ?

Fabr. spec. ins. 2. p. 485.

Spargi videtur genus Acari per totum orbem, continetque proculdubio multas species adhuc incognitas, quarum plurimæ ob parvitatem non nisi Lynceo oculo possunt discerni. Sunt tamen nonnullæ species quæ cæteras adeo mole superant ut facile etiam modico intervallo percipi possint; e. g. Acarus Ricinus Linnæi in canibus frequenter conspectus, Acarus columbarum in columbis, et acarus qui ob vividum ruborem et superficiem lanuginosam holosericus dicitur. Licet distinguantur plerique forma singulari potius quam pulchritudine,

chritudine, fpeciem tamen exoticam excipiamus necefle eft quam oftendit tabula non tantum magnitudine naturali, fed et microfcopio auctam: notas enim gerit hæc non vulgaris fplendoris; maculas fcilicet tres in corpore fuperiori, et interdum plures, colore quodam metallico velut aurato, qui fplendor præcipue notabilis, fi immerfum fuerit infectum in liquore qui vulgo dicitur *fpiritus vini*. Color imus fufco-virefcens, pallet, punctulis minimis nigris corpori impreffis. Abdominis margo leviffime crenata ferie macularum nigrarum. Caput magna ex parte conformatum eft eodem fere modo quo acari columbini, cui in hoc auratus valde videtur affinis; ope nempe roftri, cujus fuperficies inferior præcipue ferrata, uncis retro fpectantibus, animali quod vexare cupit arctiffime adhærens. Summa autem eft fimilitudo inter hanc fpeciem et Acarum Iguanæ Fabricii, quem memorat ille detectum effe mordicus affixum facculo gulari Lacertæ Iguanæ Linnæi, quæ poftea in fpiritu vini affervabatur. Simili modo auratus fe affigit Colubro Najæ Linnæi, cujus fpecimina eodem liquore condita remanent. Verifimile eft fpeciem effe novam, nifi potius varietatem effe Acari Iguanæ de quo jam diximus. Memorat Seba ferpentes interdum acaris infeftari, fed, quod vitium erat fui temporis, laxe et ambigue loquens, non acaros fed pediculos eos vocat.

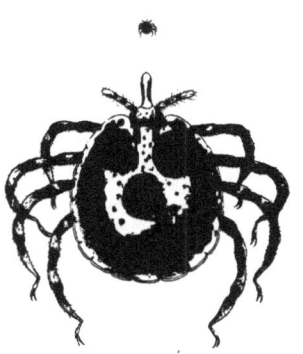

THE
GOLD-SPOTTED ACARUS.

GENERIC CHARACTER.

Eight *Legs.*
Two *Eyes,* situated on the sides of the head.
Two *Tentacula,* jointed, and shaped like feet.

SPECIFIC CHARACTER.

ORBICULAR FLATTISH ACARUS, with gold-coloured spots; the body marked above by numerous impressed points; the abdomen subcrenated.

The genus Acarus, which seems to be diffused throughout all parts of the world, and of which a great many species must doubtless remain still undiscovered, is, in general, distinguished by the extraordinary minuteness of its appearance; several kinds being scarce visible without close inspection, and easily escaping the notice of a common eye. Some species however so far exceed the rest of the genus in size as to be sufficiently conspicuous even at a moderate distance; for instance, the Acarus Ricinus or common tick, so frequently seen on dogs; the Acarus columbarum, not less plentiful on pigeons and some other animals; and the Acarus holosericeus or velvet mite, so remarkable for its bright scarlet colour and downy surface. In general the Acari are much
more

more distinguished by the singularity than the beauty of their appearance. The very curious exotic species here figured, both in its natural size and magnified by the microscope, is an exception to this general rule, and is adorned with marks of no inconsiderable splendor; the upper part of the body being furnished with three and sometimes more large spots of a golden tinge, accompanied by a metallic lustre. This appearance is however most conspicuous while the animal is immersed in spirits of wine. The general colour of this species is a pale greenish-brown, variegated with minute specks of black, forming so many impressed spots on the surface of the body. The edge of the abdomen is very slightly notched or indented by a row of marks of the same colour. In the general form of the apparatus at the head, this species bears a most striking affinity to the pigeon-tick or Acarus columbarum, being furnished like that animal, with a serrated snout, the processes of which lying on the under surface, and pointing backwards, enable it to adhere with great firmness to the skin of the creature it infests. The species to which it bears the greatest resemblance is the Acarus Iguanæ of Fabricius, which is by that author commemorated as having been found strongly affixed to the gular pouch of the Lacerta Iguana of Linnæus preserved in spirits. The present species is found adhering in the same manner to specimens preserved in spirits of the Coluber Naja or Cobra de Capello. It is most probably a new species, unless it should be regarded as a variety of the A. Iguanæ of Fabricius. The circumstance of snakes being sometimes infested by Acari is mentioned by Seba, who, in the usual inaccurate style of his time, gives them the title of Pediculi.

ALCEDO ISPIDA.

CHARACTER GENERICUS.

Rostrum trigonum, crassum, rectum, longum.
Lingua carnosa, brevissima, plana, acuta.
Pedes gressorii *plerisque*.

Lin. Syst. Nat. p. 178.

CHARACTER SPECIFICUS, &c.

ALCEDO BRACHYURA, supra cyanea, subtus fulva, loris rufis.

Lin. Syst. Nat. p. 179.

ALCEDO BRACHYURA SUBCRISTATA CÆRULEA, subtus rufa, loris fulvis, vertice nigro undulato, macula aurium gulaque albis.

Lath. ind. orn. p. 252.

ALCYON.
Gesn. av. 85.

ISPIDA.
Gesn. av. 571.
Will. orn. 101.

Non modo avium Britannicarum sed et Europæarum nitidissima est et lautissima Alcedo Ispida, exceptis Linnæi Coracia Garrula Meropeque Apiastro, quas neutras genuit

genuit Britannia, *hanc* licet advenam ad nos rariffimus cafus appulerit. Cum p fciculis vefcatur Alcedo, rivos ideo et loca impertubata quærit, folitudinis et filentii cupida; quam ob caufam melancholiæ fymbolum habetur, exemplumque egregiæ pulchritudinis protervos oculos fedulo evitantis, cuique non male convenit celeberrimi poetæ votum " Flumina amem fylvafque."

Turbata motu fertur celerrimo vix ac ne vix horrizontem fuperans, coloremque adeo vividum in tranfitu oftentat, ut alis papilionis Menelai fere æqualem diceres. Interdum fufpenfa fuper aquas alis expanfis rapideque vibratis more Nifi confpicitur, fulgores jactans tunc temporis præter folitum fplendidos. Inter ripas fluviorum, interdum etiam aquarum ftagnantium, in foraminibus alte effoffis nidificat, ova deponens quinque, feptem, vel etiam novem, Inter marem et feminam fere ambigua eft fimilitudo. Alcedo plerumque vera Halcyon creditur, quam nidum fluitantem conftruere putabant veteres; qui in hoc fortaffe errarunt, quod nidum Colymbi alicujus pro nido Halcyonis habuerint. Colymborum enim certæ fpecies nidos fluitantes e plantis aquaticis revera contexunt, qui juxta riparum aggeres inter arundines laxius fiti, fuper aquas nonnunquam a ripa huc illuc feruntur.

THE COMMON KINGFISHER.

GENERIC CHARACTER.

Bill trigonal, thick, ſtrait, long, ſharp-pointed.
Tongue fleſhy, very ſhort, flat, ſharp-pointed.
Feet (in moſt ſpecies) greſſorial, *i. e.* three toes forward and one backward, and the three lower joints of the middle toe cloſely jointed to thoſe of the outmoſt.

SPECIFIC CHARACTER, &c.

SHORT-TAILED KINGFISHER, blue above, fulvous beneath, with rufous lores and white auricular ſpot.

THE COMMON KINGFISHER.
Lath. Syn. 1. p. 626.
Will. orn. 146.

LE MARTIN-PÊCHEUR.
Buff. oiſ. 7. p. 164.
Pl. enl. 77.

The Alcedo Iſpida or common Kingfiſher is by far the moſt brilliant of the Britiſh birds: indeed no other bird of Europe can equal it in livelineſs of colours except

cept the Roller, (Coracias Garrula. Lin.) and the Bee-Eater, (Merops Apiaster. Lin.) neither of which are natives of Britain, though the former has sometimes been seen as an accidental straggler. The Kingfisher is a bird of a retired and solitary difpofition, and as from the nature of its food, (which confifts entirely of fmall fifh,) it is moft commonly found near ftreams and unfrequented places, it has therefore been fixed upon as an emblem of melancholy, and an example of dazzling beauty, in a ftate of voluntary retirement. " Flumina amem fylvafque" feems to be its motto, and it is rarely feen except in fuch fituations. If difturbed, it darts along in a rapid horizontal motion, and difplays a tranfitory glance of colour which is almoft equal in luftre to the wings of the Papilio Menelaus. Sometimes it may be feen fufpended over the ftream in the manner of a hawk, and rapidly vibrating its expanded wings, when its colour is ftill more beautifully confpicuous. The Kingfifher builds in deep holes in the banks of rivers, and fometimes of ftagnant waters. It lays from five to feven or even nine eggs. The male and female bear an extreme refemblance to each other. The Kingfifher is generally fuppofed to be the true Halcyon of the ancients, which was believed to build a floating neft. In order to account for this erroneous idea, we need only fuppofe that the nefts of fome of the Colymbi or Grebes were miftaken for thofe of the Halcyon: fome of the Colymbi do really build floating nefts of aquatic plants, &c., which though placed amongft the reeds contiguous to the banks, are yet fo loofe as occafionally to be carried to fome little diftance on the furface of the water.

GYMNOTUS ELECTRICUS.

Character Genericus.

Caput operculis lateralibus.
Tentacula duo ad labium fuperius.
Oculi cute communi tecti.
Membrana Branchioftega radiis quinque.
Corpus compreffum, fubtus pinna carinatum.
Lin. Syft. Nat. p. 144.

Character Specificus, &c.

GYMNOTUS NUDUS, dorfo apterygio, pinna caudali obtufiffima anali annexa.
Lin. Syft. Nat. p. 144.

GYMNOTUS CAUDA TRUNCATA, maxilla inferiore longiore.
Gron. zooph. 168.

GYMNOTUS NIGRICANS, cauda curta obtufa.
Seb. muf. 3. p. 108. t. 34. f. 6.
Bloch. aufl. Fifch. 2. p. 43. t. 156.

Vim illam electricam quam pro arbitrio emittere poteft Torpedo, quamque illi procul-dubio ad repellendas injurias dedit Natura, admirati funt antiqui fimul ac recentiores

recentiores physici. Tacta Torpedine, ictum illico violentum sentit hostis, probaturque ab experimentis, iisque præcipue Domini Walsh in Actis Anglicis, hunc ictum vere et omnino esse electricum, nullo modo diversum ab illo qui a machina deducitur; posseque cum plurimis, si conjunctæ sint manus, eodem temporis puncto communicari. Piscis vero quem nunc describere pergimus, vel ipsam Torpedinem vi sua electrica longe antecellit: quos enim in fluviis suis natalibus sanus valensque tetigerit, non solum motu sensuque per breve aliquod tempus privat; sed fertur insuper illos qui parum fauste in iisdem aquis nataverint, ab immodico ejus impetu subito percitos interdum periisse. Mira hac facultate vitam sustentat Gymnotus; piscesque, seu alia animalia prope ludentia quæ tactu suo obtorpuerit, corripit statim devoratque tyrannus ille quarum electricus. Paucis abhinc annis viva horum piscium specimina in Angliam illata sunt, et Londini aliisque locis publice spectabantur. Vultu est Gymnotus tetrico et injucundo, primoque intuitu anguillam magnam quodammodo repræsentat, Corpus suum vel contrahere potest vel producere; fibras nempe aliquot musculosas constringendo seu remittendo. Colore nigricat. Caput illi est crassum, corpore paulo latius, depressiusque, seu complanatum. Oculi valde exigui; Os magnum: utrisque maxillis insunt dentes parvi, acuti, numerosissimi. Circa caput, præcipue sinciput, varia sunt foramina. Totum animal muco lubrico, muco anguillæ non absimili tegitur. Squamæ illi visibiles nullæ sunt; detegi tamen fortasse possent, si cutis exsiccata et expansa esset, more cutis anguillæ. Alii sunt hujus generis pisces, qui tamen Gymnoto electrico adeo sunt absimiles ut, excepto charactere

charactere generico, cum illo nequaquam conveniant, omnique vi electrica penitus carent. Americam Auſtralem incolit Gymnotus electricus, præcipue autem in Rivo Surinam in Guiana invenitur.

THE ELECTRICAL GYMNOTUS.

GENERIC CHARACTER.

Head furnished with lateral opercula.
Two *Tentacula* at the upper lip.
Eyes covered by a skin.
Branchiostegous Membrane with five rays.
Body compressed, and carinated by a fin beneath.

SPECIFIC CHARACTER, &c.

BLACKISH GYMNOTUS, without dorsal fin; the caudal fin extremely obtuse and jointed to the anal one.

THE ELECTRICAL EEL.

The power with which Nature has armed the Torpedo, is such as to have rendered it the wonder of the ancient as well as the modern world. This power consists in a natural electricity, which is exerted at the pleasure of the animal, in such a manner as to preserve it in great measure secure from all attacks of other creatures; since no sooner is it touched than a very strong electric shock is instantly felt by the invader. That

That it *is* a real electric shock, not differing from that which is received from an electrical machine, has been clearly proved by repeated experiments; particularly by those of Mr. Walsh, related in the Philosophical Transactions; from which it appears that the shock is communicated at the same instant to a number of persons joining hands. The fish however which we now proceed to describe, is possessed of a much greater share of natural electricity than the Torpedo: so powerful is the shock which this fish, in its native rivers, and in full vigour, is capable of inflicting, that it is said to deprive almost entirely of sense and motion for some minutes, such as are exposed to its approach, and that, in consequence of this violent exertion of its electricity, it has sometimes proved fatal to such as have incautiously ventured to swim in the same water. It is by the power of electricity that the Gymnotus supports its existence: whatever smaller fish or other animals happen to approach it are instantly stupefied, and fall an easy prey to the electrical tyrant.

Some years ago some of these curious fish were brought alive from Surinam into this kingdom, and were publickly exhibited at London and elsewhere. It is a fish of a disagreeable appearance, and on a cursory view is not much unlike a large eel. Its colour is blackish, and it has a power of shortening at pleasure the length of its body, by the contraction of its muscular fibres, and again relaxing and extending itself to its former length. The head is short, somewhat broader than the body, and a little depressed or flattened: the eyes are very small; the mouth large, and both jaws are furnished with a great many very small sharp teeth.

About

About the head, especially on the fore-part, several foramina or pores appear. The whole animal is coated with a sort of mucus, not unlike that of an eel. The Gymnotus is destitute of apparent scales; but the probability is that in a dried skin prepared in the manner of an eel-skin the scales might be found.

There are some other species of Gymnoti, which differ very much in their appearance from this: they have no electric power, and are only approximated to this species by their generic character.

The Gymnotus electricus is a native of South America, and is principally found in the river Surinam in the province Guiana.

SCARABÆUS MIDAS.

Character Genericus.

Antennæ clavatæ capitulo fiffili.
Tibiæ anticæ fæpius dentatæ.

Lin. Syſt. Nat. p. 541.

Character Specificus, &c.

SCARABÆUS exſcutellatus, thorace tricorni, clypeo ſinuato bicorni.

Fab. Syſt. Ent. p. 21.
——— *Spec. inſ.* p. 24.
Gmel. Syſt. Nat. p. 1534.

Varium adeo et multiforme eſt totum ſcarabæorum genus, cornuum partiumque prominentiorum tanta eſt et fere incredibilis diverſitas, ut in iis generandis pene luſiſſe naturam putemus. Quod ſi majoribus animalibus mole æquales eſſent ſcarabæi, ipſa poetarum et pictorum monſtra, quibus quælibet audendi fingendique poteſtas, a revera exiſtentibus vincerentur. Aliis caput tantum cornutum eſt, aliis tantum thorax, aliis tum caput tum thorax. Inter rariſſimas vero ſimul ac maxime ſingulares ſpecies eminet ſcarabæus iſte in tabula, qui Americam incolit; præcipue Auſtralem? Color eſt aterrimus:

mus: corporis inferiora, præsertim versus pectus et infitiones crurum tomento obscure ferrugineo vestiuntur. Elytra seu alarum thecæ exteriores striis paucis longitudinalibus notantur. Perpulchrum rari hujus infecti specimen in Museo Leveriano conspicitur.

THE MIDAS BEETLE.

GENERIC CHARACTER.

Antennæ divided at the tip of head into several lamellæ.

Tibiæ, or second joints of the fore-legs generally toothed.

SPECIFIC CHARACTER.

NON-SCUTELLATED BEETLE, with broad treble-horned thorax and double horned sinuated clypeus.

In the beetle tribe we are presented with a wonderful, and, as it were, almost capricious diversity of form. Every variation of horn and process that imagination can conceive being exemplified in the different species of this extensive genus; and if their size approached to that of the larger animals, even the monsters of romance would be exceeded by the realities of nature. In some the head alone is horned, in others the thorax only; and in others both head and thorax are furnished with these appendages. Amongst the rarest, as well as the most singular species, may be reckoned the beetle here

here reprefented, which is a native of America, and particularly of South America? Its colour is a deep black; but the under parts, efpecially toward the breaft and the infertions of the legs, are coated with a dark ferruginous down. The Elytra or wing-fheaths are marked by a few longitudinal ftriæ. A very fine fpecimen of this rare infect is to be found in the Leverian Mufeum.

PSITTACUS MELANOPTERUS.

Character Genericus.

Rostrum aduncum: mandibula superiore mobili; cera instructa.
Nares in rostri basi.
Lingua carnosa, obtusa, integra.
Pedes scansorii.

Character Specificus, &c.

PSITTACUS pallide viridis, dorso alisque nigris, remigibus secundariis luteis apice cæruleis, rectricibus purpureis fascia nigra.
Lath. ind. orn. p. 132.

PSITTACUS pallide viridis, dorso, tectricibus alarum, caudæ fascia remigibusque primariis nigris, secundariis flavescentibus cæruleo-punctatis.
Gmel. Syst. Nat. p. 350.

Psittacus Melanopterus, coloribus elegantissimis uberrime ornatus, insulam Javam inhabitat, in Batavia præcipue conspectus. In tabula exprimitur avis magnitudine prope naturali. In museis rarissima est hæc species. Specimen ipsissimum, unde hæc nostra figura depicta est, in Museo Britannico asservatur.

K

THE BLACK-WINGED PARRAKEET.

GENERIC CHARACTER.

Bill hooked. Upper mandible moveable.
Nostrils round, placed in the base of the bill.
Tongue fleshy, broad, blunt at the end.
Legs short. Toes formed for climbing, viz. two forward and two backward.

SPECIFIC CHARACTER.

PALE-GREEN PARRAKEET, with black back and wings; the secondary wing-feathers yellow tipped with blue; the tail lilac-coloured and crossed by a black bar.

PERRUCHE à ailes variées.
Buff. 6. p. 172.

PETITE PERRUCHE de Batavia.
Pl. enl. 791. f. 1.

The Psittacus melanopterus, so remarkable for the elegance of its colours, is a native of the island of Java, and is found at Batavia. The plate represents it nearly of its natural size. It is a species very rarely seen in collections. The beautiful specimen from which this figure was executed is in the British Museum.

BALÆNA MYSTICETUS.

Character Genericus.

Dentium loco in maxilla superiore laminæ corneæ. *Fistula* duplex.
Lin. Syst. Nat. p. 105.

Character Specificus, &c.

BALÆNA naribus flexuosis in medio capite, dorso impinni.
Lin. Syst. Nat. p. 105.

BALÆNA dorso impinni, fistula in medio capite, dorso caudam versus carinato.
Gron. zooph. 139.

BALÆNA vulgaris edentula, dorso non pinnato.
Raij. pisc. p. 16. & 6.

BALÆNA vera Rondeletii, *et* Balæna Rondeletii, Gesneri et aliorum.
Will. pisc. p. 38. 35.

Licet ob formæ externæ similitudinem et vitam æquoream videatur fortasse inter pisces et animalia cetaria commune esse quoddam cognationis vinculum, revera tamen *mammalia aquatica* habenda sunt. Utcunque

que enim corporis figura, quodque pedibus carere putentur, a reliquis quadrupedibus primo visu longe discrepent, sunt tamen iis revera pedes, quamvis non extrinsecus visibiles; cum habeant pinnæ duæ anteriores ossa iis analoga quibus instruuntur pedes antici cæterorum quadrupedum, quibus vero postici, ea contineant duæ posteriores, quæ in cauda quasi coadunatæ pinnam unicam horizontalem videntur efficere. Similis quoque est partium internarum conformatio ac in aliis mammalibus, pulmonum scilicet, intestinorum, &c. Tepet præterea sanguis, ut in illis, feminæque pullos lacte alunt. Tanta est in omnibus cetariis characterum generalium similitudo, ut in uno genere fere reponi possent. Ut vero species facilius dignoscerentur, Linnæo et omnibus fere physicis recentioribus placuit illa in quatuor genera dividere, quæ notis secundariis, situ nempe dentium, fistularum in capite, aliisque signis distinguuntur, quæ vocantur *Monodon, Balæna, Physeter, Delphinus.* Horum in præcipuis Balæna et Physetere continentur species maximæ. Omnium princeps est Balæna Mysticetus, quo sane majus monstrum nec mare nec tellus generat, ni verum sit quod de Krakene narratur. Antequam numerum redegisset balænarum, quem jam optime callent septentrionales populi, capiendi modus, conspecti sæpius sunt Mysticeti longitudine centum pedum. Raro nunc dierum videntur qui pedes sexaginta superant. Mysticeto vix excogitari possit aliud animal rudius et informius. Constat enim fere tertia pars e capite. Os monstrose amplum. Lingua interdum pedes octodecim seu viginti longa. Oculi pro corpore minutissimi. In maxilla superiore sitæ sunt numerosissimæ laminæ corneæ serie æquali dispositæ, quæ vulgo *os cetaceum*

cetaceum vocantur. Per fiſtulam, quæ duplex in ſummo capite, quaſi columnam aquæ in altum aſſurgentem incredibili vi eructat. Color communis eſt livide albido-cinereus, dorſo pinniſque obſcurioribus et fere ſubnigricantibus. Variat autem ut et alia pleraque animalia, colore plus minuſve ſaturato. Habitat ut plurimum, in maribus ſeptentrionalibus, ibique arte omnigena in ejus perniciem conſpiratur: in merce enim eſt oleum cetarium. Victitat præcipue Meduſis, Sepiis, aliiſque ejuſmodi.

Dolendum eſt poetas, utcunque legentium animos ſuavitate delectent, et percellant ſublimitate, in deſcribendis iis quæ ad hiſtoriam naturalem ſpectant epitheta adeo inſcite ſeligere, ut ipſam rei de qua canunt imaginem ſæpius a vero detorqueant. Hoc nullibi manifeſtius quam in deſcriptione illa, grandi certe et magnifica, quæ apud Miltonum legitur balænæ dormientis, cui tamen adjungitur epitheton falſum omnino et incongruum.

―――――――――― " horrida ponti
Bellua, quæ fluctus inter mirabile Monſtrum
Navigat, æquoreæque exultat maxima gentis.
Olim hæc noctivagæ rectori viſa biremis,
Norwegii ſalis in ſpuma dum forte quieſcit,
(Sic perhibent nautæ) vaſta inſula creditur, amplo
Immenſum porrecta ſinu; latus anchora prenſat
Squamoſum, et tuta fruitur ſtatione Magiſter,
Dum pontum obvelant tenebræ, luxque alma moratur."
Parad. amiſſ. lat. reddit. a Dobson.

Nulli autem in toto genere contingunt ſquamæ. At ſi forte me putet aliquis hypercriticum, et voluiſſe Miltonum balænam non vere ſquamiferam, ſed ſuperficiem tantum

tantum habentem rudem et scabrosam, qualis scilicet est cortex arboris, huic opinioni invitus assentiar: quod enim illum in errorem duxerit non e longinquo petendum, figura nempe in Gesneri operibus, quæ pravissime efficta quasi magnis squamis vestita videtur, cuique præterea inscribitur " Nautæ in dorso Cetorum, quæ insulas putant, anchoras figentes, sæpe periclitantur." Vix possit dubitari quin poeta nostras celeberrimus, qui multifaria imbutus scientia, librorum quasi gurges erat et helluo, Gesneri scriptis, grandi tunc temporis scientiæ naturalis thesauro, optime esset versatus, quodque balæna imago quam ibi viderat altius in animo inhæserat.

THE
MYSTICETUS,
OR
GREAT NORTHERN WHALE.

Generic Character.

No *Teeth*, inftead of which are fituated horny laminæ in the upper jaw.

A double *Fiftula* or fpiracle on the top of the head.

Specific Character, &c.

TOOTHLESS WHALE, blackifh above, white below, without dorfal fin.

The COMMON or GREENLAND WHALE.

The COMMON WHALE.
Pennant. Arct. Zool. fup. 101. n. 5.

The WHALEBONE WHALE.
Phil. tranf. abr. 7. p. 424.

The cetaceous animals, however nearly approximated to fifhes by external form and refidence in the waters, are in reality to be confidered as aquatic quadrupeds: for though from their general fhape and feeming want

of

of feet they appear at first view widely removed from the rest of the Mammalia, yet these parts really exist, though not outwardly visible; the two anterior fins being furnished with bones like the feet of other quadrupeds, and the two posterior ones (which from their situation, appear to form but one horizontal caudal fin,) containing the analogous bones of the two hind feet. All the internal parts of this tribe of animals are likewise formed on the same plan as in other Mammalia: having similar lungs, intestines, &c. They have also warm blood, and the females, like other quadrupeds, suckle their young. The general characters of all the Cetacea are so similar, that, in an enlarged view, they might all form one great genus; but as this perhaps would not facilitate the distinction of the several species, Linnæus and most other modern naturalists have agreed in dividing the cetaceous animals into different genera, distinguished by secondary characters, as the situation of the teeth and of the spouting-hole or fistula on the head. This distribution admits of four distinct genera, viz. *Monodon, Balæna, Physeter, Delphinus.* Of these the genera of Balæna and Physeter are the two principal, and contain the largest animals. The Balæna Mysticetus, or great northern Whale, is as it were the chief of the whole tribe, and (unless the Kraken be not a fabulous existence,) is the largest of all known animals either of land or sea. Before the northern whale-fisheries had reduced the number of this species, it was no very uncommon circumstance to find specimens of an hundred feet in length. These are now rarely seen, and it is not often that they are found of more than sixty feet.

In

In its general shape and appearance this animal is peculiarly uncouth; the head constituting nearly a third of the whole mass. The mouth is of prodigious amplitude; the tongue sometimes measuring eighteen or twenty feet in length. The eyes most disproportionably small. In the upper jaw is a vast number of very long horny laminæ disposed in regular series: these are popularly known by the name of whale-bone. On the top of the head is a double fistula or spout-hole, through which the enormous animal discharges the water at intervals, causing the appearance of a marine jet d'eau ascending to a great height in the air. The general colour of this species is a pale whitish ash, deeper on the back and fins, (where indeed it is nearly blackish.) Like most other animals, however, it varies in intensity of colour. Its general residence is in the northern seas, where it has long constituted the principal trade of the whale or oil fishery. Its food consists chiefly of different species of Sepiæ, Medusæ, &c.

It is to be lamented that in the poetical descriptions of various striking scenes in natural history, the epithets by which many objects are distinguished are, for want of due knowledge of the subject, improperly chosen, and utterly inconsonant with the character of the things intended; by which means the description, however beautiful in point of language, fails in point of accuracy. This is no where more strikingly illustrated than in the august lines of Milton, in which the description of a sleeping whale is injured by an epithet of all others the least according with the nature of the animal.

———————— " that sea-beast
Leviathan, which God of all his works
                Created

Created hugest that swim th' ocean stream:
Him, haply slumb'ring on the Norway foam,
The pilot of some small night-founder'd skiff
Deeming some island, oft, as seamen tell,
With fixed anchor in his scaly rind,
Moors by his side under the lee, while night
Invests the sea, and wished morn delays."

None of the cetaceous tribe are furnished with scales, or any thing analogous to them. It must be acknowledged however that this observation may appear in no small degree hypercritical, and that Milton by the expression of *scaly rind* might only mean rough or scaly in the same sense that those epithets are applied to the bark of a tree, or any irregular surface. There can be little doubt however that real and proper scales were intended by the poet; nor is it difficult to discover the particular circumstance which impressed Milton with this erroneous idea, viz. a figure in the works of Gesner, so injudiciously expressed as to appear on a cursory view as if coated with large scales, with a vessel near it with harpooners, &c. over which is the observation of sailors often mistaking a whale for an island, and thus endangering themselves by attempting to anchor on it. As the general learning and extensive reading of our great poet are so well known, it can hardly be doubted that he was conversant with the writings of Gesner, whose work was then the great depository of natural knowledge, and that the figure and description there given left a lasting impression on his mind.

CERAMBYX LONGIMANUS.

Character Genericus.

Antennæ attenuatæ.
Thorax spinosus aut gibbus.
Elytra linearia.

Lin. Syst. Nat. p. 621.

Character Specificus, &c.

CERAMBYX thorace spinis mobilibus, elytris basi unidentatis apiceque bidentatis, antennis longis.

Lin. Syst. Nat. p. 621.

SCARABÆUS CAPRICORNUS maximus nigricans, fasciis elytrorum coccineis et flavis.

Sloan. jam. 2. p. 209.
Merian Surin. t. 28.
Aubent. Pl. Enl. 64. f. 1.

Cum ad genus *Cerambyx*, quo nescio an ullum aliud contineant Coleoptera mirabilius, numerosissimæ referantur species; perpaucæ tamen sunt quæ longimanum vel magnitudine vel colorum pulchritudine possunt superare. In tabula depingitur hoc insectum magnitudine naturali. Americæ Australis est incola. Elytrorum color

color primarius eft fufcus, feu potius nigricans, ftriis maculifque fubflavis et aurantiis, et in nonnullis fpeciminibus, fubrubris interftinctus. Caput etiam cum thorace fimili modo variatur; cruraque eodem colore fafciata. Elytrorum fuperficies propius confpecta villo feu tomento breviffimo veftitur. Speciem hanc præcipue diftinguunt crura antica ultra folitum producta; quæ tamen longiora funt mari quam feminæ. Cerambyces, ut et alia Coleoptera, ab ovis oriuntur, larvarumque mutationes fubeunt, quæ plerumque albo-flavefcunt, et in putridis arborum truncis potiffimum degunt.

THE LONG-LEGGED CERAMBYX.

GENERIC CHARACTER.

Antennæ attenuated.
Thorax either spinous or gibbous.
Elytra linear.

SPECIFIC CHARACTER, &c.

BLACKISH CERAMBYX with elytra fasciated with red and yellow, with very long forelegs and antennæ.

NOCOONACA.
Grew. muf. p. 163. t. 13.

L'ARLEQUIN DE CAYENNE.
Pl. enl. 64. f. 1.

The genus Cerambyx, one of the most curious in the whole tribe of coleopterous insects, contains a prodigious number of species; many of which are extremely remarkable for the singularity of their appearance. There are however few which can exceed in this respect the species here represented, which is also one of the largest of the genus, and is highly distinguished

by

by the beauty of its colours. The figure shews it of its natural fize. It is a native of South America: the ground-colour of the elytra or wing-cafes is a brownifh black, varied with ftreaks and markings of pale yellow and orange, which in fome fpecimens approaches to red. The head and thorax of the infect are alfo marked in the fame manner, and the legs are croffed by a band of the fame colours. The furface of the wing-cafes, when narrowly viewed, is of a velvetty appearance, or coated with a fine upright villus. This fpecies is principally diftinguifhed by the great length of the fore-legs, which are ftill longer in the male infect than the female. The Cerambyces, like other infects of the beetle-tribe, proceed from eggs, and pafs through the ftate of larvæ, which are generally of a yellowifh white colour, and principally refide in the decayed parts of trees.

AMPELIS GARRULUS.

CHARACTER GENERICUS.

Rostrum rectum, convexum: Mandibula superiore longiore, subincurvata, utrinque emarginata.
Lingua acuta, cartilaginea, bifida.

Lin. Syst. Nat. p. 297.

CHARACTER SPECIFICUS, &c.

AMPELIS occipite cristato, remigibus secundariis apice membranaceo colorato.

Lin. Syst. Nat. p. 297.

GARRULUS BOHEMICUS.

Gesn. av. 703.
Will. orn. 90. t. 20.

LANIUS GARRULUS.

Fn. Suec. 2. n. 82.

Frequens licet reperiatur bella hæc avis in variis Europæ temperatioris partibus, nos non nisi fortuita advena invisit, idque præcipue si hyems fuerit frigidior. Ingenio est vivido admodum alacrique, et ut tandem inusitatam formæ elegantiam, nota sibi fere peculiari distinguitur, cui simile vix in alia ave Europæa possit observari,

observari, remigum nempe secundariorum appendicibus, quæ corneæ, planæ, oblongæ, lucidæ, et ruberrimæ. Colores feminæ languidiores. Magnitudine alaudam communem paulo superat Ampelis Garrulus, et fructibus baccisque præcipue vescitur.

THE BOHEMIAN CHATTERER.

GENERIC CHARACTER.

Bill ſtrait, a little convex above, and bending towards the point; near the end of the upper mandible a ſmall notch on each ſide.
Noſtrils hid in briſtles.
Middle Toe cloſely connected at the baſe to the outmoſt.

Pennant.

SPECIFIC CHARACTER, &c.

CRESTED CHATTERER, with the ſecondary wing-feathers tipped by horny red appendages.

THE BOHEMIAN CHATTERER.
Will. orn. p. 132. pl. 20.
THE SILK-TAIL.
Ray. Syn. p. 85. A.
THE WAXEN CHATTERER.
Br. Zool. No. 112. pl. 48.

This beautiful bird, though common in many of the temperate parts of Europe, is but an occaſional viſitant in our own country, into which it ſometimes migrates,

grates, particularly during a fevere winter. It is of a moſt lively and active difpofition, and is diſtinguiſhed, exclufive of the general elegance of its form, by a particularity fcarce to be obferved in any other European bird, viz. the extraordinary formation of the ſhorter or fecondary wing-feathers, which are tipped by oblong, flat, horny appendages of a lucid furface and of a bright vermilion-colour. The colours of the female are lefs brilliant than thofe of the male. Its fize is fomewhat larger than that of a lark. This fpecies feeds principally on fruits and berries.

LIMAX ATER.

CHARACTER GENERICUS.

Corpus oblongum, repens; fupra clypeo carnofo; fubtus Difco longitudinali plano.
Foramen laterale dextrum pro genitalibus et excrementis.
Tentacula quatuor, fupra os.
Lin. Syft. Nat. p. 1081.

CHARACTER SPECIFICUS, &c.

LIMAX ATERRIMUS fubtus pallidus.
LIMAX ATER.
Lift. Angl. 131.
LIMAX tota nigra.
Aldr. inf. 702.
COCHLEA NUDA 3 tota nigra.
Gefn. aquat. 254.
LIMAX ATER.
Lin. Syft. Nat. p. 1081.

LIMAX MAXIMUS.

CHARACTER SPECIFICUS, &c.

LIMAX CINEREUS atro maculatus.
LIMAX MAXIMUS cinereus ftriatus.
Lift. anat. t. 3. f. 6—10.
LIMAX MAXIMUS.
Lin. Syft. Nat. p. 1081.
LIMAX CINEREUS. β.
Gmel. Syft. Nat. p. 3100.

Nudum

Nudum est genus Limax caretque testa. De hoc differere supervacaneum fortasse nonnullis videatur, quippe quod vulgatissimum non possit ignorari. Dignissimum tamen est genus quod speciatim describatur, cum exstet exemplum generale seu archetypum unde omnes fere testarum univalvium incolæ formantur; quorum nonnulli adeo Limaci similes, ut primo visu in hoc tantum differre videantur quod se ad libitum intra testam possint subducere. Exemplo sit genus *Helix* dictum, in quo nempe continentur Helices vulgares testaceæ. Quinimo reliquæ univalves (exceptis paucis quæ insigniter discrepant) ad genus *Limax* plus minus appropinquant. Specierum Britannicarum notiores sunt Limax ater, et Limax maximus: quorum prior aterrimo colore facillime distinguitur, in pratis et pascuis sæpissime repertus; alter rarior, fusco-pallens, non sine maculis striisque inæqualibus nigerrimis, in sylvis præcipue conspicitur, nec raro in hortis vere et autumno: in domos etiam irrepit. Convenit utrisque de victu, foliis scilicet et radicibus plantarum. Limax maculatus, (ut et alii nonnulli,) acaris minimis super corpus turmatim discurrentibus, et in ipsum etiam foramen laterale thoracis irrepentibus sæpissime solet infestari. Vetat tamen torpidum ingenium, aut mucus quo obducitur corpus, ut signa det molestiæ et perturbationis, vel exeuntibus acaris, vel intrantibus.

THE
BLACK LIMAX.

Generic Character.

Body oblong; Thorax convex or fhielded above, flat beneath; with a *Foramen* on the right fide. Four *Tentacula,* fituated above the mouth.

Specific Character, &c.
JET-BLACK LIMAX, pale beneath.
THE BLACK SLUG.
THE COMMON BLACK SNAIL.

THE
SPOTTED LIMAX.

Specific Character, &c.
GREYISH LIMAX, fpotted with black.
THE GREAT SPOTTED SLUG.
THE SPOTTED WOOD-SNAIL.
THE SPOTTED HOUSE-SLUG, or CEL-
LAR-SNAIL.

The genus Limax or Slug, confifts of the naked or fhell-lefs Snails. As thefe animals are fo very common, it might feem almoft unneceffary to introduce them

into

into a work like the prefent. The genus however is in reality of very great importance, fince it ftands, as it were, the general archetype or pattern on which the animals of almoft all the univalve fhells are formed: indeed fo very nearly are fome of them allied to this genus, that they feem, on a curfory view, to differ in fcarce any other circumftance than that of being furnifhed with fhells, into which they can at pleafure withdraw themfelves. Of this the genus Helix, which contains the common or fhell-fnails, is a convincing proof. The reft of the univalves, (with a few remarkable exceptions,) are more or lefs fimilar to the genus Limax. Two of the moft familiar fpecies of Limax which this country produces are the Limax ater and maximus: the one is diftinguifhed by its intenfe blacknefs, and is extremely common in fields and meadows; the other, lefs common than the former, is of a pale brown, with irregular deep-black fpots and ftreaks: it is principally feen in woods and in garden-ground during the vernal and autumnal feafons, and not unfrequently creeps into houfes. Both agree in their mode of living; feeding on the leaves and roots of vegetables. The fpotted Slug, like fome others of its genus, is often infefted by a very fmall fpecies of acarus, which appears in great numbers, running with much celerity over the animal, and frequently entering the lateral foramen of the body. The Limax however, either from its natural hebetude, or from being coated at all times by a quantity of mucus, feems to feel no particular inconvenience from thefe little infects, and fhews no fymptoms of irritation even when they are running in and out of the orifice in its fide.

GRYLLUS CITRIFOLIUS.

Character Genericus.

Caput inflexum, maxillofum, palpis inftructum.
Antennæ fetaceæ s. filiformes.
Alæ quatuor, deflexæ, convolutæ: inferiores plicatæ.
Pedes poftici faltatorii: *Ungues* ubique bini.

Lin. Syft. Nat. p. 692.

Character Specificus, &c.

GRYLLUS thorace tetragono angulis fcabro.
Lin. Syft. Nat. p. 695.
LOCUSTA VIRIDIS.
Degeer. inf. 3. p. 437. n. 7. t. 37. f. 3.
LOCUSTA CITRIFOLIA. L: thorace tetragono angulis crenatis.
Fabr. fp. inf. 2. p. 356.

Gryllorum omnium quotquot continet genus elytris quafi foliatis diftinctos, maxima fortaffe eft hæc fpecies, folioque fimillima. Varias Indiæ Orientalis partes incolit.

THE
CITRON-LEAVED LOCUST.

GENERIC CHARACTER.

Head inflected, armed with jaws, and furnished with palpi or feelers.
Antennæ either fetaceous or filiform.
Wings four, deflex, convolute: the inferior ones plaited.
Feet hinder formed for leaping: *Claws* on all the feet double.

SPECIFIC CHARACTER.

LOCUST with the thorax of a fomewhat quadrangular form and crenated on the edges, with very large green leaf-like exterior wings

---

Of all that tribe of the genus Gryllus diftinguifhed by the leaf-like appearance of the elytra or exterior wings, this feems to be the largeft fpecies. It alfo yields to none in the perfect and ftriking refemblance to leaves which its wings exhibit. It is a native of various parts of India.

PARUS CÆRULEUS.

CHARACTER GENERICUS.

Rostrum integerrimum, basi setis tectum.
Lingua truncata, setis terminata.

Lin. Syst. Nat. p. 340.

CHARACTER SPECIFICUS, &c.

PARUS virescens, subtus luteus, remigibus cærulescentibus, fronte alba, vertice cæruleo.

PARUS remigibus cærulescentibus : primoribus margine exteriore albis, fronte alba, vertice cæruleo.

Lin. Syst. Nat. p. 341.

PARUS CÆRULEUS.

Gesn. av. 641.
Will. orn. 175.
Raj. av. 74.

Licet inter pulcherrimas avium Britannicarum merito numerari possit Parus cæruleus, detrahit tamen a pretio quotidianus conspectus. Fatendum etiam est inesse illi indolem minus aptam ad conciliandum favorem; non tantum enim gemmas arborum frugiferarum devastat, fed et audax eft ultra molem. Univerfo fane generi ingenium eft minime mite et amabile; ferunter enim aliis avibus vim inferre et occidere cerebrum evellendo, quod folent comedere. Hoc licet frequenter fieri vix aufim dicere, a fedulis tamen hiftoriæ naturalis indagatoribus affirmatur. Paris omnibus mira eft in nidificando folertia; foecunditafque ultra fidem. Ifte de quo jam loquimur nidum ftruit elegantem in cavis arborum, vel fub murorum fummitatibus, interdum etiam in tuguriis et ftabulis. Ova duodecim, quindecim, et etiam octodecim deponit; parturit tamen, ut plurimum, non nifi femel in anno.

THE BLUE TITMOUSE.

GENERIC CHARACTER.

Bill ſtrait, a little compreſſed, ſtrong, hard, and ſharp-pointed.
Noſtrils round, and covered with reflex briſtles.
Tongue as if cut off at the end, and terminated by three or four briſtles.
Toes divided to their origin; back toe large and ſtrong.

SPECIFIC CHARACTER, &c.

GREENISH-BACKED TITMOUSE, yellow beneath, with bluiſh remiges, white forehead, and azure crown.

THE BLUE TITMOUSE.
  Will. orn. p. 242. pl. 43.
  Br. Zool. 1. No. 163. pl. 57. fig. 2.

LA MESANGE BLEUE.
  Pl. enl. 3. fig. 2.

Amongſt the moſt beautiful of the Britiſh birds may be numbered the Parus cæruleus or common blue Titmouſe, which, from its frequent appearance, is leſs regarded

garded than fo elegant a visitant would otherwise be. It has however some qualities which are not calculated to obtain it universal approbation; since it is not only destructive to the young buds of fruit-trees, but has also a certain audacity in its disposition which would hardly be expected from so small a bird: indeed the manners of the Pari in general are observed to be not the most amiable, and they are accused of sometimes attacking other birds, and killing them by picking out their brains. Whether this can be considered as a frequent occurrence I cannot take upon me to determine, but it is recorded by some of the most accurate observers of Nature. The birds of this genus eminently excel in nidification, and are prolific almost beyond belief. The present species builds its curious nest in holes of trees; under the eaves of walls, and sometimes in out-houses. It lays about twelve, fifteen, and even sometimes eighteen eggs, but seldom breeds more than once in a year.

PENNATULA RENIFORMIS.

CHARACTER GENERICUS.

Corpus in aliis pinnatum, in aliis integrum.
Stipes nudus offiiculo interno.

CHARACTER SPECIFICUS, &c.

PENNATULA RENIFORMIS, altero latere polypifera, ftipite lumbriciformi.
Pall. el. zooph. p. 374. n. 222.

PENNATULA RENIFORMIS, ftirpe lumbrici facie, altero latere polypifera.
Soland. et Ellis zooph. p. 65. n. 8.

ALCYONIUM AGARICUM.
Gmel. Syft. Nat. p. 3811.

Formofiffimæ huic Pennatulæ diverfa eft facies a plerifque congeneribus. E ftipite qui brevis vermique fimilis, exoritur corpus expanfum, reniforme, fupra foraminibus tubulatum, unde ad libitum extenduntur tentacula, feu membra hydras referentia. Color in parte fuperiori viget lætiffime purpureus; in inferiori pallidior eft, et interdum fere flavefcens. In infulis Americæ variis innafcitur pennatula reniformis, nec raro circa littora confpicitur.

THE KIDNEY-SHAPED PENNATULA.

GENERIC CHARACTER.

Body in some species pinnated, in some entire; with polypes proceeding from its upper surface, and having a naked stem, furnished with an internal bone.

SPECIFIC CHARACTER, &c.

KIDNEY-SHAPED PENNATULA with worm-like stem.

THE KIDNEY-SHAPED PURPLE SEA-PEN.

Phil. Transf. vol. 53. t. 19. fig. 6—10.
Soland. and Ellis zooph. p. 65.

This most beautiful Pennatula is to be ranked amongst those species which recede in point of habit from the major part of the genus. It consists of an expanded, kidney-shaped, flattened body, rising from a short worm-like stem, and covered on the upper surface with numerous tubular orifices, through which are exserted at pleasure the tentacula or polype-formed limbs

limbs of the animal. The colour of the upper surface is a beautiful purple; of the lower less brilliant, and sometimes yellowish. It is a native of the West-Indian Islands, where it is not uncommon.

ZEUS IMPERIALIS.

Character Genericus.

Caput compressum, declive: *Labium superius* membrana transversa fornicatum. *Lingua* subulata.

Membrana branchiostega radiis septem perpendicularibus: infimo transverso.

Corpus compressum.

Lin. Syst. Nat. p. 454.

Character Specificus, &c.

ZEUS cauda sublunari, corpore nunc rubente, nunc viridi, nunc purpureo, albo-guttato.

ZEUS LUNA?

Gmel. Syst. Nat. p. 1225.

POISSON DE LUNE?

Du Hamel des pêches, 3. p. 74. t. 15.

ZEUS cauda bifurca, colore argenteo purpureo splendens.

Strom. Sondmor. 323, 325. t. 1. f. 20.

Specierum omnium, quas paucas continet genus, maximam longe et splendidissimam depinximus, reliquos sane pisces Europæos vividis coloribus vincentem; quibus nitet adeo cum recens capta sit, ut insignes fulgores

gores imitando aſſequi incaſſum conetur ars pictoria. Variat præterea color primarius, qui vel ruber vel viridis aureo ſplendore quaſi vernice obducitur. Totum corpus, excepto ventre, maculis plurimis ovatis argenteo-albis guttatum eſt. Pinnæ, ut plurimum, coccineæ. Cauda latiſſima admodum lunata. Repertus eſt Zeus imperialis in Europæis multis littoribus, rarius in Britannicis. Creſcere ſolet in magnam molem, nec defuit ſpecimen quod tres pedes longitudine, pondere centum fere libras æquaret. Notandum vero eſt alios pleroſque piſces quos complectitur genus, modicos eſſe ſi non parvos, nitide argenteos, inſignes latis corporibus, forma tenui et compreſſa, radioſque nonnullos pinnarum quæ in dorſo caudaque, longius ultra reliquos excurrere.

THE
OPAH,
OR
IMPERIAL ZEUS.

GENERIC CHARACTER.

Head compressed, sloping down: *Upper lip* arched by a transverse membrane. *Tongue* subulate. *Branchiostegous membrane* with seven perpendicular rays; the lower transverse. *Body* compressed.

SPECIFIC CHARACTER, &c.

ZEUS with somewhat lunated tail: the body generally either red, green, or purple, with oval white spots.

OPAH OR KING-FISH.

Phil. Transf. abr. XI. p. 879. t. 5.
Brit. Zool. III. p. 195 t. 42. f. 2.

Of all the species of this genus, which is not a numerous one, the fish here delineated is by far the largest as well as the most splendid in its colour: it may indeed

indeed be confidered as the moſt ſuperb of all the European fiſh, and when recently taken exhibits an appearance ſo ſingularly vivid as to ſurpaſs all the attempts of art to give an adequate idea of its beauty. It alſo varies in this reſpect; the predominating colour being either red or green, with a rich luſtre of gold, and appearing as if varniſhed. The whole body, except on the belly, is ſprinkled with numerous oval ſpots of a ſilvery white. The fins are commonly ſcarlet. The tail is very broad and ſtrongly lunated. This moſt elegant fiſh is ſometimes found on the Britiſh coaſt, but is more frequent on thoſe of other parts of Europe. It grows to a very large ſize, having been ſeen of the length of three feet, and of the weight of an hundred pounds. It may not be improper to obſerve that moſt of the other fiſhes of the genus, except the Doree, are ſmall ſpecies, remarkable for their ſhining ſilvery colour, the great breadth of their bodies, their thin or compreſſed form, and the length of ſome of the rays of their dorſal and caudal fins, which frequently run out far beyond the reſt.

VULTUR PERCNOPTERUS.

Character Genericus.

Rostrum rectum, apice aduncum.
Caput impenne, antice nuda cute.
Lingua bifida.
Lin. Syst. Nat. p. 121.

Character Specificus, &c.

VULTUR remigibus nigris margine exteriore (praeter extimas) canis.
Lin. Syst. Nat. p. 123.

VULTUR (percnopterus) capite nudo, gula plumosa.
Hasselq. it. 209.

FALCO MONTANUS ÆGYPTIACUS.
Hasselq. act. stockh. 1751. p. 196.

VULTUR SACER ÆGYPTIUS.
Aldr. av. 1. p. 378. t. 379.

De avidissima horum alitum voracitate copiosius disserere longum esset et supervacaneum. Norunt omnes inexplebilem fere esse iis cupiditatem edendi. Non tamen

tamen inopportunum fit notare paucos præter Condoram seu vulturem maximum Americanum, animalia viva mortuis anteponere, sed cadavera diligenter quærere quæ mira narium sagacitate e longinquo sentiunt. In orientalibus regionibus variæ vulturum species exercituum motus comitantur, juxtaque fatales campos gregatim circumvolant, dapem e strage orituram avide expectantes. Longam tamen passæ esuriem, præter solitum voraces quicquid cibi fors obtulerit subito et audacter arripiunt. Narrat Dominus Bruce peregrinator celeberrimus, dum iter Abissinum perageret, et in monte qui Lanalmon dicitur, cum sociis jam jam pransurus esset, vulturem immanem e proximis rupibus magna vi in patinam insiliisse, et cum coxa armoque caprinis simul arreptis avolasse : mox reducem et plus prædæ meditantem scloppeto ab ipso interfectum fuisse. Aquilam vocat hunc alitem Dominus Bruce, sed a figura et descriptione satis patet vulturem fuisse, barbatum scilicet Linnæi, mole et gula jamdudum insignem. Non possum non suspicari Symphalidas veterum majoribus vulturini generis speciebus originem debere. Vultur Percnopterus non tantum in calidioribus regionibus invenitur, sed et in Europa temperata. Figura hæc nostra ab ipsa ave fideliter delineata est.

THE ALPINE VULTURE.

GENERIC CHARACTER.

Bill ſtrait, hooked at the tip.
Head commonly bare of feathers, with a naked ſkin in front.
Tongue bifid.

SPECIFIC CHARACTER, &c.

VULTURE with black remiges, hoary on the outer edge (except the exterior ones.)

THE VULTURINE EAGLE OF ALDROVAND.
Will. orn. p. 64. t. 4.

LE VAUTOUR DES ALPES.
Briſſ. orn. 1. p. 464. t. 4.

LE PERCNOPTERE.
Buff. ois. 1. p. 149.
Pl. enl. 426.

The voracity and predacious diſpoſition of the birds of this tribe are too well known to require particular deſcription. It may be obſerved, however, that moſt of the ſpecies prefer the fleſh of dead animals to other prey;

prey; few, except the Condor, or great South American vulture, attacking any living animals in preference, but diligently seeking for the remains of carrion, which they are enabled to perceive from a wonderful distance by their exquisite power of scent. In the Eastern climates vultures of various species never fail to attend the field of battle, eagerly hovering in multitudes at some distance, in expectation of their wished-for banquet. When pressed by hunger, they become unusually rapacious, and seize with indiscriminating haste whatever food is accessible. Thus we are assured by the celebrated Mr. Bruce, that during his Abyssinian expedition, while himself and his companions were seated on the top of the mountain Lanalmon, preparing their repast, a large vulture came from the neighbouring cliffs, and seized out of the vessel in which their meat lay, a leg and shoulder of goats flesh in its talons, and flew away with them both; and soon returning for a second booty, was shot by Mr. Bruce. From the description and figure given by that gentleman, it appears probable, that though called an Eagle, it was a species of vulture; viz. the vultur barbatus of Linnæus, which is one of the largest of the genus, and is a bird of great strength and vigour. It is no improbable supposition that the attacks of such birds may have afforded some foundation for the ancient fictions of the Stymphalides. The vultur percnopterus is found not only in the hotter regions of the world, but even in the temperate parts of Europe. The figure here represented was taken with great accuracy from the bird itself.

LACERTA BASILISCUS.

Character Genericus.

Corpus tetrapodum caudatum, nudum.
Lin. Syst. Nat. p. 359.

Character Specificus, &c.

LACERTA cauda tereti longa, pinna dorsali radiata, occipite cristato.

Lin. Syst. Nat. p. 366.
Laur. amph. p. 50. n. 75.
Seb. mus. 1. t. 100. f. 1.

Basiliscus, quem memorant antiqui animalium venenosissimum, vivit non nisi in bellis pictorum et poetarum fabulis. Omissis aliis, Lucanum satis sit citare, qui licentia sisus vere poetica describit eum ardenti in Africa horrendum sibilantem, et torvo lumine ipsum etiam serpentinum genus procul a seipso deterrentem.

" Sibilaque effundens cunctas terrentia pestes,
Ante venena nocens, late sibi submovet omne
Vulgus, et in vacua regnat Basiliscus arena."

Basiliscus autem, quem eo nomine norunt nunc temporis physici, est lacertæ species forma admodum singulari,

lari, quæque eminenter diſtinguitur cute velut in alæ formam expanſa, per totum dorſum et maximam caudæ partem continuata, intuſque radiata, qualiter fere ſunt piſcium pinnæ, ſeu ut rectius loquar, alæ *draconis* ſive *lacertæ volantis*; quæque inæqualiter aſſurgit in variis partibus, adeo ut ſinuoſa et denticulata videatur, et ad arbitrium vel erigitur et dilatatur, aut deprimitur et contrahitur. Occiput intus cavum quaſi in cucullum ſeu potius in criſtam extenditur. Viſu licet terribilis ſit Baſiliſcus, ingenio tamen eſt prorſus innocuo. Aliarum plurimarum lacertarum more, inter arbores verſatur, inſectis aliiſque ejuſmodi victitans. Americam Auſtralem incolit. Jamdudum in Sebæ theſauro depictus eſt eleganter admodum et fideliter; effecit autem forma nova et incognita (rariſſima enim eſt ſpecies) ut a multis pro monſtro imaginario haberetur. Extat tamen in Muſeo Britannico ſpecimen perfectiſſimum, ſpiritu vini conditum, quod Sebanæ figuræ veritatem abunde comprobat. Probabile porro eſt, immo pene certum, Linnæum, qui, teſtante filio, ipſum animal nunquam viderat, ab hac Sebæ figura deſcriptionem ſuam ſpecificam condidiſſe. Color Baſiliſci pallet fuſco-cinereus, corpore ſuperiore notis ſeu umbris aliquot obſcurioribus variato. Longitudo ei eſt quaſi ſeſquipedalis. Notandum eſt, juniorem cutis iſtius quæ porrigitur ſuper dorſum caudamque nec non criſtæ quæ in occipitio aſſurgit, levia tantum veſtigia oſtendere.

THE
BASILISK.

Generic Character.
Body four-footed, tailed, naked.

Specific Character, &c.
LONG-TAILED LIZARD, with radiated dorsal and caudal fin, and pointed occipital crest.

THE BASILISK.

The Basilisk of the ancients, supposed to be the most malignant of all poisonous animals, and of which the very aspect was said to be fatal, is a fabulous existence, to be found only in the representations of painters and poets. Without citing other descriptions, it may be sufficient to quote that of Lucan, who, with true poetic licence, represents the Basilisk exerting his terrific glance in the burning deserts of Africa, and obliging the rest of the poisonous tribe to preserve an humble distance.

" Sibilaque effundens cunctas terrentia pestes,
Ante venena nocens, late sibi submovet omne
Vulgus, et in vacua regnat Basiliscus arena."

But

> But fiercely hissing, thro' the poison'd air
> The Basilisk exerts his deathful glare:
> At distance bids each vulgar pest remain,
> And reigns sole monarch of his sultry plain.

But the animal known in modern natural history by this name is a species of lizard, of a very singular shape, and which is particularly distinguished by a long and broad wing-like process or expansion continued along the whole length of the back, and to a very considerable distance on the upper part of the tail, and furnished at certain distances with internal radii analogous to those in the fins of fishes, or still more so to those in the wings of the draco volans or flying lizard. This process is of different elevation in different parts, so as to appear strongly sinuated and indented, and is capable of being either dilated or contracted at the pleasure of the animal. The occiput or hind part of the head is elevated into a very conspicuous pointed hood or hollow crest. Notwithstanding its formidable appearance the Basilisk is a perfectly harmless animal, and like many other of the lizard tribe, resides principally amongst trees, where it feeds on insects, &c. It is a native of South America. It has long ago been admirably figured by Seba, and as it is an extremely rare species, has sometimes been considered, (from the strangeness of its form) as a fictitious representation. There is however in the British Museum a very fine specimen, well preserved in spirits, and which fully confirms the excellency of Seba's figure; from which, in all probability, Linnæus himself, (who never saw the animal,) took his specific description. The

The colour of the Basilisk is a pale cinereous brown, with some darker variegations towards the upper part of the body. Its length is about a foot and half. The young or small specimens have but a slight appearance either of the dorsal or caudal process, or of the pointed occipital crest.

PES DIDI.

EX PEDE HERCULEM!

Didum ineptum Linnæi, miram scilicet et anomalam avem, in priore numero hujus operis fideliter ad exemplar archetypum depictam descripsi. At de vera avis existentia a multis semper dubitatum est, eoque magis quod adhuc credi solitum est nulla ejus in museis Europæis reperiri posse vestigia. Dum autem in miscellaneam farraginem et quisquilias Musei Britannici nuperrime obiter inspiciebam, comite ingenioso pictore domino Reinagle juniore, fauste admodum se oculis obtulit pes adeo insolitus ut primo visu Didi pedem nobis illico in mentem revocaverit. Examinato dehinc ulterius specimine, verum esse et genuinum Didi pedem satis constabat. Dubium autem omne sustulit Grewii descriptio in opere quod dicitur " Museum Regalis " Societatis," cui eum plene et ad amussim respondere sensi. Figuræ igitur, quæ juxta naturam depingitur, adjunxi etiam descriptionem quæ apud Grewium legitur, occasionem avide arripiens rem rarissimam diuque desideratam lectoribus proponendi.

" Qui ibi asservatur pes squamis flavo rubescentibus
" contegitur, et longitudine paululum superat quan-
" tuor uncias, latitudine quinque, saltem circa arti-
" culos; et licet minor sit pede struthionis et casuarii,
" forsan tamen fere æquali sit robore, si ratio habeatur
" brevitatis."

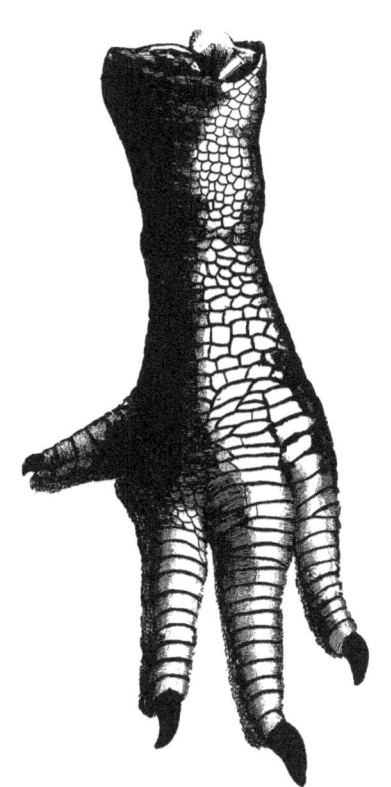

THE LEG OF A DODO.

In a preceding number of the prefent work I have given a defcription, accompanied by a figure accurately copied from an original picture faid to have been taken from nature, of that moft fingular bird called the Dodo: an animal fo very rare, and of an appearance fo uncouth, as to have given rife to fome doubts as to its real exiftence; which was alfo rendered ftill more fufpicious from the fuppofed want of any remains of the bird itfelf in the mufeums of Europe. A very fhort time fince however, on curforily examining feveral mifcellaneous articles in one of the apartments of the Britifh Mufeum, in company with that very ingenious artift Mr. Reinagle jun', we had the good fortune to difcover a leg, which even at firft view appeared of fo peculiar an afpect that it inftantly fuggefted the idea of the bird in queftion. On farther examination it was ftill lefs to be doubted that it muft really have belonged to that curious bird; and on collating it with the defcription given by Grew in his Mufeum Regalis Societatis, it agreed in all points with the meafurements there particularized. I therefore accompany the figure, here given, which is reprefented of the natural fize, with the defcription from the above work of Grew, and it is with peculiar pleafure that I embrace the opportunity of prefenting my readers with fo interefting a curiofity.

" The

"The leg here preserved is covered with a reddish
"yellow scale. Not much above four inches long;
"yet above five in thickness, or round about the
"joints: wherein though it be inferior to that of an
"Ostrich or Cassoary, yet joined with its shortness,
"may render it of almost equal strength."

TESTUDO MELEAGRIS.

Character Genericus.

Corpus tetrapodum, caudatum, testa obtectum. *Os* mandibulis nudis, edentulis.

Lin. Syst. Nat. p. 350.

Character Specificus.

TESTUDO pedibus subpalmatis? testa ovata glabra maculis innumeris flavis guttata.

Plurimas testudinum species sibi invicem nimis affines accurate dignoscere difficillimum est. De aliis ne dubitari quidem possit, quippe quæ notas gerant conspicuas et insignes ad distinctionem: qualis scilicet est testudo geometrica, quam striarum flavarum super scutum bella et ordinata serie vel tiro statim agnoverit. Illam etiam quam describere pergimus a reliquo genere satis sejungit notabilis characterum et colorum dispositio. Longa est, ut plurimum, quinque vel sex uncias. Color fusco-castaneus saturatior per totum corpus superius guttulis ovatis albido-flavescentibus pulcherrime aspergitur, in singula tegminis divisione quasi ducenis. Scutum læve est, carens sulcis et prominentiis, nisi quod per medium trium præcipuarum divisionum excurrat carina paululum levata, quæ tamen in nonnullis speciminibus

minibus obfcurius cernitur. Lævis etiam eft margo fcuti, feu ex partibus conftans una ferie continuatis, non inæqualiter ferratis, fed figuram prope ellipticam toto ambitu efficientibus. Superficies inferior flavefcit maculis aliquot fufcis et inæqualibus notata. Caput modicum. Oculi magni. Pedes iis fimiles quos habent reliquæ teftudines terreftres et fluviatiles, unguibus muniuntur validis. Cauda longula et fquamofa. Si fuper fundum nigriorem confluxerint inter fe maculæ, quod rarius evenit, perit magna ex parte pulchritudo teftudinis mcleagridis. In America præcipue innafcitur.

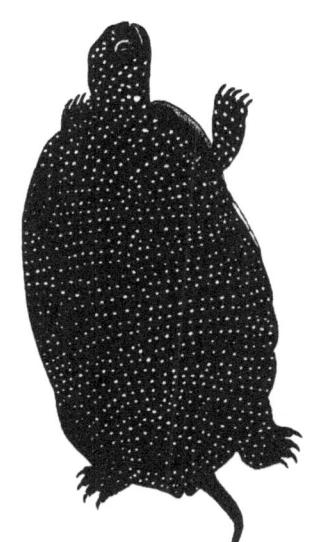

THE
SPECKLED TORTOISE.

GENERIC CHARACTER.

Body four-footed, tailed, covered with a shell.
Mouth consisting of naked toothless mandibles.

SPECIFIC CHARACTER, &c.

TORTOISE with subpalmated? feet, and ovate smooth shell speckled with innumerable yellow dots.

LA JAUNE.
Cepede Hist. Nat. des quadr. ovip. 1. p. 135. t. 6.

So great is the similarity between several of the tortoise tribe, that it is by no means easy to distinguish with accuracy the particular species. Some however are so strongly characterized as to be at all times readily ascertained. Thus the Testudo geometrica or striped Tortoise is so strikingly distinguished by the beautiful and regular disposition of the yellow marks on its shield, as to be instantly recognised by any one in the least conversant with this genus. The species here represented is also, in general, so remarkable in its appearance as to be immediately known from any other kind. Its usual length is about five or six inches: its colour a deep chesnut-brown, most elegantly marked over the whole upper surface with innumerable oval specks of yellowish white. There are scarce less than 150 or 200 of these specks on each division of the shield. The whole is smooth, or undistinguished by any furrows or risings on the divisions, except that down the middle of the three chief or central pieces runs an elevated or projecting carina as it were, which is much less distinct in some specimens than in others. The edge or outline of the shell is smooth, or composed of pieces which do not project unequally, but form one continued, nearly eliptic figure. The lower surface is pale yellowish, with a few irregular patches of brown. The head is moderately large. The eyes large. The feet of the usual structure in other land and fresh-water tortoises, and furnished with strong claws. The tail longish and scaly. It sometimes happens that the beautiful appearance which generally distinguishes this species, is nearly lost, or at least greatly obliterated, by the dark ground-colour predominating too much, and the spots becoming confluent. This however is not often the case. It is a native of America.

DORIS ARGO.

Character Genericus.

Corpus repens, oblongum, fubtus planum.
Os antice fubtus.
Anus poftice, fupra cinctus ciliis.
Tentacula duo, fupra corpus antice, intra foramina retractilia.

Character Specificus, &c.

DORIS OVALIS, corpore lævi, tentaculis duobus ad os, ano ciliato phrygio.
Lin. Syst. Nat. p. 1083.

ARGO.
Bohadsch. mar. 65. t. 5. f. 45.

LEPUS MARINUS alter major.
Column. ecphr. t. 32.

Plurima quæ hoc genus amplectitur animalia limacibus valde affinia omnino in mari degunt. Oftendit tabula fpecierum Europæarum maximam et formofiffimam. Color variat: interdum fcilicet flavus eft, plus minufve faturatus; interdum aurantius, feu etiam coccineus. In multis Britanniæ littoribus non raro confpicitur Doris Argo.

THE LEMON DORIS.

GENERIC CHARACTER.

Body repent, oblong, flat beneath.
Mouth placed below, toward the anterior end.
Vent behind, surrounded above by a fringe.
Tentacula two, seated on the upper part of the body in front, retractile.

SPECIFIC CHARACTER, &c.

OVAL DORIS with smooth body; the vent surrounded by a ramified fringe.

LEMON DORIS.
Pennant Brit. Zool. 4. p. 36.

THE SEA-LEMON.

The animals of this genus are greatly allied to those of the genus Limax, but are entirely marine. The species of Doris are numerous. The largest as well as the most elegant of the European kinds is that figured on the annexed plate. In colour it varies much; being sometimes of a yellow, more or less deep, and sometimes of a bright orange, or even scarlet. It is not unfrequently found on several parts of the coasts of Britain.

SPONGIA INFUNDIBULUM.

CHARACTER GENERICUS.

Animal? fixum, flexile, polymorphum, torpidiſ-
ſimum, contextum vel e fibris reticulatis,
vel e ſpinulis gelatina viva veſtitis;
Oſculis ſeu foraminibus ſuperficiei aquam reſpiran-
tibus.

Soland. et Ellis zooph. p. 182.

CHARACTER SPECIFICUS, &c.

SPONGIA infundibuliformis turbinata flexilis.
Lin. Syſt. Nat. p. 1296:
SPONGIA forma infundibuli.
C. Bauh. pin. p. 369.
J. Bauh. hiſt. pl. 3. p. 816.
SPONGIA foliata aſpera et Spongia infundibuli-
formis.
Petiv. peregr. t. 9. f. 4. 6.
SPONGIA (crateriformis) infundibuliformis mol-
liuſcula, membranaceo-celluloſa, extus vil-
loſa craſſior.
Pall. el. zooph. p. 386. n. 233.

De ſpongiarum natura, mira certe et ambigua, diu
patuit philoſophis amplus diſputandi campus. Credi-
derunt

derunt nonnulli satis inepte, quæque opinio nunc penitus abolevit, esse eas vermium quorundam opus qui in cavitatibus pererrantes reperiuntur. Alii mera esse vegetabilia putarunt. Inesse autem iis vim vitæ ex hoc satis constat, quod in aquis natalibus attrectatæ a tactu paululum refugiant, quodque quiescentes poros alternatim contrahant et dilatent. Ut verbo dicam, constant spongiæ e ramosissima tuborum capillaceorum copia, facultatem quandam contractionis habentium: horum ope nutrimentum ex aquis in quibus crescunt absorbentes. Iis igitur utpote *zoophytorum* omnium inertissimis seponendus est locus proprius et ab aliis separatus. Facie inter se plurimum differunt. Aliæ scilicet *amorphæ*, seu figura carentes certa et constanti, ut spongia *officinalis* vel vulgaris. Aliæ cyathi instar formatæ. Aliæ tubulatæ; aliæ multiformes; aliæ denique ramosæ et etiam reticulatæ ad similitudinem quodammodo accedunt Gorgoniæ, seu Flabelli Veneris. Species, quam pro exemplo depinximus, maris Mediterranei et Indici rupibus, more reliqui generis, adhæret. Magnitudine variat. Habet nempe interdum diametros pedem, ad minimum, interdum paucas tantum uncias. Color ejus leviter fuscus, et substantia minus tenax quam spongiæ vulgaris, quæ et *officinalis* dicitur.

FUNNEL SPONGE.

GENERIC CHARACTER.

Animal? fixed, flexible, torpid, of various forms; composed either of reticulated fibres, or masses of small spines interwoven together; clothed with a living? gelatinous flesh full of small mouths or foramina on its surface, by which it sucks in and throws out the water.

SPECIFIC CHARACTER, &c.

FUNNEL-SHAPED FLEXILE SPONGE with surface more or less irregular or roughened.

CUP SPONGE.

FUNNEL SPONGE.

Sponges have afforded a field of controversy for philosophical observers, and may be numbered amongst the most obscure or doubtful productions of nature. By some they have been supposed the fabric of certain worms allied to Terebellæ, which are often found straying about in their cavities: an idea not very probable, and which is now sufficiently exploded. Others have

have imagined them to be mere vegetables; but that they are really poffeffed of a living principle is evident from the circumftance of their alternately contracting and dilating their pores, and fhrinking in fome degree from the touch when examined in their native waters. In fhort, fponges confift of an infinitely ramified mafs of capillary tubes, poffeffed of a certain degree of contractile power, and capable from their ftructure, of abforbing nutriment from the furrounding fluid in which they are by nature immerfed. They therefore form an animal tribe different from all others, and may be confidered as the moft torpid of all Zoophytes. The different fpecies of Sponge differ greatly in appearance from each other: fome being amorphous, or of no regular fhape, as the common or officinal fponge: others cyathiform or cup-fhaped: others tubular, and of various forms; and fome are ramified and reticulated in fuch a manner as to bear a confiderable refemblance to the fea-fan or Gorgonia Flabellum of Linnæus. The fpecies here exhibited, as an example of the genus, is found both in the Mediterranean and Indian feas; adhering, like others of its genus, to rocks. In fize it varies from a few inches in diameter to that of a foot or more. Its colour is a pale brown, and its fubftance lefs ftrong or tenacious than that of the common or officinal fpecies.

INDEX.

Pl.	
128.	ACARUS auratus.
129.	Alcedo Ispida.
135.	Ampelis Garrulus.
133.	Balæna Mysticetus.
134.	Cerambyx longimanus.
122.	Coluber Cerastes.
117.	Crax Alector.
123.	Didus ineptus.
145.	Doris Argo.
121.	Gordius aquaticus.
115.	Gryllus laurifolius.
136.	Gryllus citrifolius.
130.	Gymnotus electricus.
142.	Lacerta Basiliscus.
137.	Limax ater & max'.
119.	Mantis siccifolia.
118.	Madrepora Cerebrum.
112.	Medusa Infundibulum
114.	Motacilla hirundinacea
138.	Parus cæruleus.
143.	Pes Didi.
113.	Papilio Nestor.
125.	Papilio Ripheus.
124.	Pennatula argentea.
139.	Pennatula reniformis.
126.	Picus erythrocephalus.
111.	Pipra punctata.
132.	Psittacus melanopterus.
127.	Rana arborea.
131.	Scarabæus Midas.
146.	Spongia Infundibulum.
120.	Tantalus ruber.
144.	Testudo Meleagris.
116.	Trigla cataphracta.
141.	Vultur Percnopterus.
140.	Zeus imperialis.

INDEX.

Pl.	
128.	ACARUS gold-spotted
142.	Basilisk.
131.	Beetle Midas.
113.	Butterfly Nestor.
125.	Butterfly Ripheus.
134.	Cerambyx long-legged.
135.	Chatterer Bohemian.
117.	Curasso common.
123.	Dodo.
143.	Dodo leg.
145.	Doris Lemon.
127.	Frog tree.
116.	Gurnard mailed.
130.	Gymnotus electrical.
121.	Hair-worm.
120.	Ibis scarlet.
129.	Kingfisher common.
115.	Locust bay-leaved.
136.	Locust citron-leaved.
118.	Madrepore Brain.
111.	Manakin speckled.
119.	Mantis dry-leaf.
112.	Medusa Funnel.
140.	Opah, or imperial Zeus.
132.	Parrakeet black-winged.
124.	Pennatula silver.
139.	Pennatula kidney-shaped.
137.	Slug black, and spotted.
146.	Sponge Funnel.
138.	Titmouse blue.
144.	Tortoise speckled.
122.	Viper horned.
141.	Vulture Alpine.
114.	Warbler Swallow.
126.	Woodpecker red-headed.
133.	Whale great Northern.

www.ingramcontent.com/pod-product-compliance
Lightning Source LLC
Chambersburg PA
CBHW021816230426
43669CB00008B/765